PINCUSHIONS

Pincushions

Averil Colby

B T Batsford Ltd   London & Sydney

This paperback edition published 1988
ISBN 0 7134 5880 1

Filmset by Keyspools Limited, Golborne, Lancashire
Printed in Great Britain by
The Bath Press, Bath
for the publishers B T Batsford Ltd,
4 Fitzhardinge Street, London W1H 0AH

Contents

Acknowledgement

The length of this acknowledgement is no measure of my gratitude to everyone who has helped me with the research, advice, loans, photographs and time which have gone to make up this book.

For the loan of their pincushions, permission for photographs to be taken and much advice, I am especially grateful to Mrs R. A. Burtt, Mrs Valerie Cliffe, Mrs Marian Collins, Miss Joan Edwards, Mrs Karen Finch, Mrs Hugh Foster, Mrs Mary Hillier, Miss Phoebe Leicester, Mr David Lewis, Mrs Mark Lubbock, Miss Katharine Pleydell-Bouverie, Mrs Olive Pass and the Dorset Federation of Women's Institutes, Miss Helen Rhodes, Miss Muriel Rose, Miss Constance Sidney-Smith, Miss A. H. St Johnston, Mrs Dorothy Tod, Mrs Stanley Trickey, Mrs Oscar Truscott, Mr Roger Warner and Mrs Katharine Yates. Also the Directors of the Victoria and Albert Museum and Miss Santina Levey, the Museum of Costume, Bath and Mrs Myra Mines, the American Museum in Britain and Mrs Gonin, to Messrs Spink and Mr W. H. Harvey for the gift of the photograph on page 10, and the R. B. Kay-Shuttleworth collection at Gawthorpe Hall.

For invaluable help with drawings and photographs, I am equally indebted to Miss Jeanette Perree, Mrs Dorothy Jones, Mr and Mrs Newton-Clare and Mr Sebastian Cliffe.

My thanks to Mr Samuel Carr for his kind help and patience are all the more unqualified for my awareness of the danger of taking them for granted, when I am late again with a script.

The cover shows a cream satin maternity pincushion of 1854 (*Museum of Costume, Bath*).

Introduction

Pincushions do not seem to need much introduction, as they must be among the most familiar of household things, although things have changed since 1911, when 'hardly any room is thought completely furnished without a pincushion of some kind'.

Pincushions cannot compare for showmanship with embroidered hangings or church vestments, but at their best they can equal in miniature the highest skill given to more notable pieces of work.

In the past they have been considered suitable as gifts for all occasions and all people from Queen Elizabeth I to a Victorian baby, and as a single item taken from the needlework of the last 400 years at least, they illustrate the whole needlework history of that period. Someone once said, that 'we can penetrate into the past more easily through the small things that people have loved, than through the great', and certainly the work put into some pincushions must have been the labour of love or they would not have been made at all.

The cost is so small that it is not worth considering. Most materials can be found in a rag-bag, literally 'remnants of remnants', or bought for a few pence. A pincushion can be made in a short time, and although a handful or two of bran in a calico bag no doubt will serve the purpose, with a little time and trouble, and pride in the work, there is no reason why it should not be a small masterpiece of skill.

1 Late sixteenth- or early seventeenth-century pincushion embroidered with silk and metal threads

History

The history of the present-day pincushion began long before metal pins were made. Early pins were sharp thorns, and fish and animal bones, all of them fragile enough to need protection when not in use. Possibly they were pinned to, or enclosed in, a piece of soft skin, which developed into the thorn cases used by North American Indians. Their original use most likely was to fasten clothing of some kind, also undoubtedly of skin.

It is known that by the 1300s small cases were being made to house pins and needles, so that they could be carried on the person or in a pouch or purse; and although few have survived, many later cases which are made of bone, ivory and silver, have done so. Usually they are cylindrical, and known variously as pincushion boxes, pin-poppets or pin-cases.

At the end of the sixteenth century mention is made of pin-pillows, the first indication of the now familiar cushion type of pin holder. All were finely embroidered on linen, satin or canvas.

By this time also, pins were sufficiently plentiful for them to be kept in large pincushions on the dressing table, as well as having a supply to carry in case of need during the day.

2 Eighteenth-century pincushion box with a pad of blue velvet

3 Embroidered blue satin pincushion said to have belonged to Queen Elizabeth I. The cover material suggests that it may have been re-covered about the end of the seventeenth or beginning of the eighteenth century

8

From about the 1590s and into the seventeenth century, embroidered draw-string purses were carried, and often small hanging pincushions worked with a matching pattern were attached to them with a cord.

4 Seventeenth-century drawstring purse embroidered with coloured silk and metal threads, with a hanging pincushion

5 Seventeenth-century drawstring purse, with similar embroidery and the pincushion in the shape of a bunch of grapes to match the embroidered pattern

Also during the seventeenth century, sets of dressing table silver were made, in which a silver-mounted pincushion was included, either surmounting the lid of a trinket box, or on its own stand. Other dressing table pincushions in the eighteenth century, were mounted on the lids of wooden boxes, some of which contained a small drawer beneath the cushioned top for trinkets or a little sewing equipment.

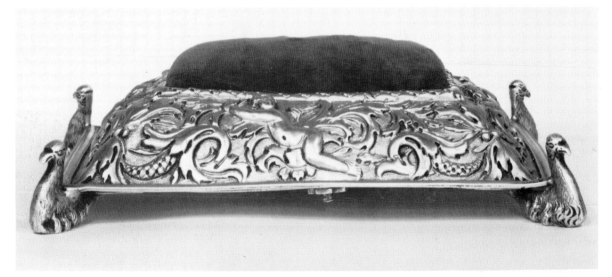

6 Silver mounted pincushion of the time of Charles II, *c.* 1680

7 Early eighteenth-century trinket box with drawer. The cushion top, padded with wool and horsehair, has been re-covered

8 Eighteenth-century American silver-mounted pin-ball

Hanging pincushions had a long and fashionable career after the seventeenth century. Some were of jewelled gold, but more usually they were of embroidery of one kind or another, and by the eighteenth century the covers were worked also with needle weaving and knitting in fine silk and with patchwork. Most were rounded in shape and known as pin-balls, some of which were silver mounted for hanging, but others were hung with cord or ribbon.

During the eighteenth century pincushions were used for political propaganda in connection with the 1745 rebellion. Some covers made of satin were printed with the names of those who had died and inscribed 'MART. FOR K. & COU 1746'. Others had the words 'GOD PRESERVE P.C. AND DOWN WITH THE RUMP' which had been woven into garter lengths and then pieces joined and stuffed as pincushions, which women and girls wore hanging from their garters.

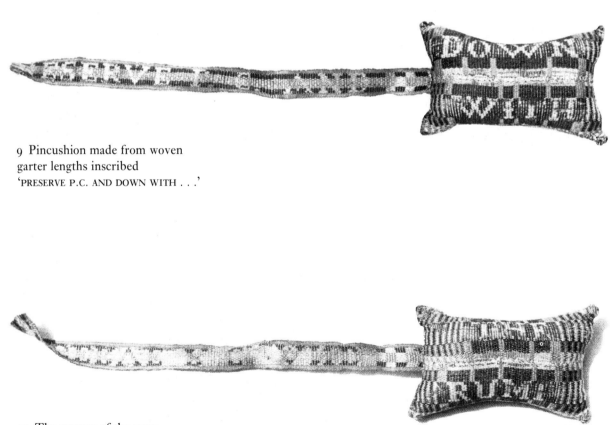

9 Pincushion made from woven garter lengths inscribed 'PRESERVE P.C. AND DOWN WITH . . .'

10 The reverse of the same cushion with the words 'THE RUMP'

11 Nineteenth-century pin-wheels decorated with paintings of daisies and a rural scene

Other historical events were commemorated in commercially-made pincushions, which were popular souvenirs of any event from a family wedding to the death of a national hero. The death of the Duke of York on 5 January 1837 was noted on several flat pin-wheel pincushions inscribed 'THE SOLDIER'S FRIEND'. Likewise Queen Caroline, on whose death mourning pincushions were sold in the streets for 4d each.

Pin-wheels were carried in the reticule or pocket when pin-balls were not worn. Decoration was light; bead work, ribbon work and other embroidery, and hand painting on silk were typical. Other pocket and purse pincushions were made of wood, ivory, mother-of-pearl, Tonbridge Ware, and leather.

Pin-stuck cushions were made from the seventeenth to the nineteenth centuries. Their decoration was made entirely of pins, which cannot be removed without spoiling the pattern. They had considerable social significance, especially in the etiquette of courtship, marriage and maternity. Suitably inscribed love tokens were exchanged between young couples, others were included in trousseaux and a layette was considered incomplete without a maternity pincushion, no matter what the class or social standing of the parents of the infant.

Beads were popular as decoration, either sewn on or pinstuck by putting a pin through each, but the cushions were of little use, as it was impossible to get a pin into some, and in others equally impossible to get one out, without spoiling the pattern.

12 Cream velvet pincushion with glazed black paper corners inscribed with poker work and black ink 'QUEEN CAROLINE DIED AUG^t 7 1821'

13 Nineteenth-century
bead-embroidered and pinstuck
cushion made by North American
Indians

14 Pocket, Purse and Work-box pincushions
top left White leather with red velvet ribbon
top centre Ebony with silver initial
top right Ivory with blue satin ribbon
middle left Tonbridge Ware with red velvet ribbon
middle right Mother of pearl with scarlet silk ribbon
bottom left Knitted cover
bottom right Mother of pearl butterfly

The cult of the nineteenth-century parlour formed a satisfying outlet for the making of pincushions which had no other purpose than to be hung on the wall or kept on occasional tables.

15 Coal scuttle and a basket for the table

16 Some hanging pincushions for the Victorian parlour wall

Real egg-cups of silver or china were fitted with pincushions, as were also all manner of ornamental china, wood, glass and metal objects.

17 Blue and white jug decorated with maroon and white beads

18 Silver egg cup with velvet cushion

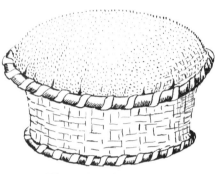

19 Blue velvet pincushion in a small basket

20 Silver-mounted frog pincushion, hallmarked 1907

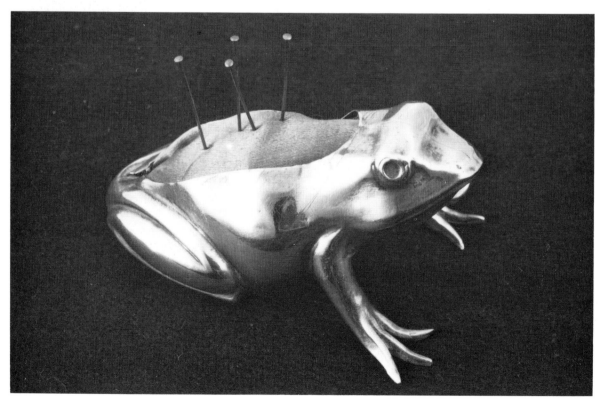

In spite of the apparent silly season of pincushion making at the end of the nineteenth century, many more were made which were of fine work and others which were attached to practical aids to sewing. There were many versions of the clamp pincushion, which could be screwed to the table, to make a 'third hand' for sewing. The material to be run or hemmed could be pinned to the cushion at one end of the seam, leaving both hands free. Weighted pincushions made to stand on the table served the same purpose, and other types were made as aids to dressmaking.

21 Turned wood clamp with fitted pincushion. The top can be removed and a thimble kept in a hidden recess

22 Philadelphia Sewing Bird, with a metal clamp, fitted with a bird on a spring clip, so that material can be held in the beak

Present-day pincushions are all made at home. With the exception of a card pin-wheel, it is not possible to buy a serviceable pincushion; not even a shell decorated souvenir. But fine examples of craftsmanship can be bought as mounts for pincushions although not for everyday use. The embroidery and other skills used to make the everyday cushion are still to be found and there are signs quite recently of a revival of the nineteenth-century love tokens, so perhaps the practice of making pincushions as gifts is also being revived.

23 Pillow cushion of fine knitted lace, with an under cover of pink sateen

Materials

Stuffings and fillings

The stuffed pad or cushion part of a pincushion is not only basic to its function, but it affects also the kind of decoration planned for the top cover. The choice of shape for a pincushion is unlimited, but the most usual are:

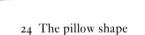

24 The pillow shape

25 The flat mattress

26 The box cushion

There are different ways of making a pad for each.

Two kinds of stuffing material are generally used – granular or fibrous – but others, which really are stiffeners or weights, are paper, vilene, buckram, card or lead.

27 Pincushion stiffened with paper or thin card

Granular fillings

The most suitable are bran, sawdust and emery powder, and as a rule, an under cover is made separately to hold them. All must be very dry before using, especially emery powder, as pins and needles put in to clean, will rust and certainly will not 'clean themselves' if left in, as some believe. At one time, doll pincushions which hung on the wall were made with their legs filled with emery powder.

Moths are addicted to bran and not averse to sawdust, but cedar dust, sometimes obtainable from a cabinet maker or carpenter, is supposed to deter them. A quick spray with a fly-killing aerosol before stuffing, will help to do this also.

Fibrous stuffings

These are the most commendable. Woollen materials are the best as they are a safeguard against rust, although not against moth, but a fly-spray will help again.

Natural, unprocessed sheep's wool, collected from hedgerows, fences and so on, is good for stuffing pillow shaped and other soft cushions, but it must be washed to remove dirt and oil, and carded or teased out to get rid of thorns, twigs and tangles. Sheep's wool should be scissor-cut before stuffing with it, otherwise it is difficult to pack in firmly. Other woollens to use are unravelled knitting or crochet, which also should be cut up, and woven woollen fabrics, such as scraps of worn blanket or tweed, unravel well for stuffings.

28 Hanging doll pincushion, the legs stuffed with emery powder

29 Sheepswool, before and after scissor-cutting

Remnants of other woven wool fabrics, such as flannel, tweed, unworn blanket, art felt and table felt, can be stitched together in layers and trimmed to shape to make flat pads for box and mattress types of pincushions.

A good pad for a round cushion is made by cutting strips of flannel, flannelette or art felt, and rolling them until the required size is made.

Synthetic materials, such as acrilan and terylene wadding can be used, but really, 'there is no substitute for wool' in pincushions. It is a myth that thistledown can be used; it is no good at all.

Foam rubber disintegrates, and flock and cotton wool (except rarely) are hard and lumpy and should not be used.

30 Materials suitable as stuffings: worn blanket, scraps of tweed, unravelled wool, rolled flannel, pad of flannel pieces, table felt, new blanket

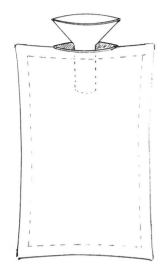

31 Funnel for fine granulated fillings

Aids to stuffing

A small, wide-necked funnel saves spilling when using fine granulated fillings like sawdust and so on.

A stuffing stick as used by toy-makers, or an old-type wooden butcher's skewer, smoothed and slightly blunted at one end, should be used for packing in fibrous fillings.

After being stuffed with sheep's wool, a pincushion should be left overnight in a warm place, such as a cylinder cupboard. The warmth will expand the wool slightly and firm the cushion.

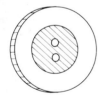

32 Stuffing stick for packing fibrous fillings

Weights and stiffeners

Tailor's weights can be attached to pincushions to prevent them moving when in use. They can be attached to the outside or sewn to the inside of the under cover before stuffing, through the two holes in the centre.

Small bags of shot can also be sewn into the under cover.

Card, tailor's canvas or buckram can be used to stiffen the base and sides of some box cushions, or the top and base of pincushions made like a sandwich, in which a pad is sewn between them.

Paper or thin card is used to stiffen nearly all the 'fancy' patchwork pincushions, such as the star shapes.

Pin-wheels consist almost entirely of covered, card discs sewn together, but many have a circle of flannel between them and the pins are held at the edges.

33 Tailor's weight

Cover materials

Under covers for holding stuffings should be strong enough to do so properly. Slightly used and washed materials often take pins more easily than new stuffs, and calico (bleached or unbleached), linen, flannelette and close cottons, such as good sateen, can be used. Coloured materials should be tested for fastness, especially when used under open work, or transparent tops.

Pink, blue or maroon sateen often was used under knitted lace.

Granular fillings need close fabrics, as they disintegrate in use and may leak through anything loosely woven.

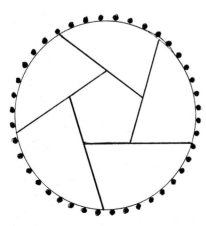

34 Patchwork pin-wheel

Top cover materials are almost unlimited in choice and sources of supply. As long as the quality and condition are good, it does not matter whether they come new from a shop, or from the piece-bag, and either way, a small amount only is needed for a pincushion. Of proven worth are linen, cambric and lawn; nearly all cottons such as twill, calico, chintz, sateen, fine piqué and muslin; silk and satin, including ribbons and brocades; velveteen and velvet, except chiffon velvet, but an old top hat provides ideal silk velvet; embroidery canvas, and fine soft leather such as kid: and all may be patterned or plain, whether suitable for dress or furnishings.

Some drip-dry cottons are rather tough to take pins easily, but muslin and lawn have proved to be tougher than they seem. A short close-pile velvet should be used but the choice is endless.

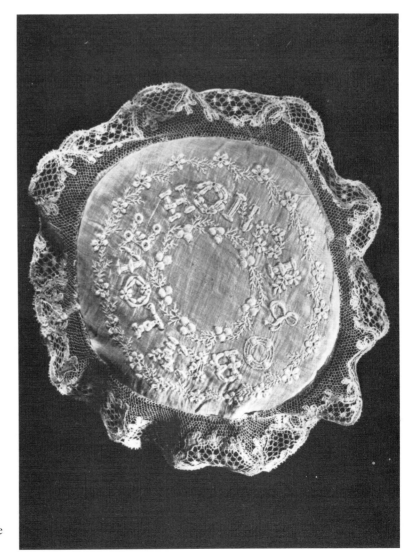

35 An English nineteenth-century Wedding Pincushion. A round cushion with a muslin top embroidered in white with flower and leaf garlands and edged with lace. The inscription 'LOVE HONOR & OBEY' is embroidered between the garlands

Threads

Sewing thread for hems and joins, whether hand or machine-stitched, should be related in kind to the material: cotton for cotton materials, linen thread for linen, silk for silk and satin, and nylon or terylene for similar synthetic materials. There are, of course, no hard-and-fast rules and in most cases 'common sense must prevail'.

36 An eighteenth-century pillow pincushion, made from embroidered scraps of satin

Embroidery threads, or those which can be used for embroidery (in couching for example), are almost unlimited in choice. Usually they are for decoration only, but when fastenings also are part of the decoration, then a thread of appropriate strength is needed. The choice of thread naturally must be related to the stitches, but the 'working surface' of a pincushion needs to be smoothly embroidered, or not embroidered at all. The threads (and stitches) used, are given for each pincushion illustrated and include linen, stranded cotton, crochet threads, sewing silk, buttonhole twist, tapestry and knitting wools, and lurex, when the piece-bag or jumble sale fails with silver or silver-gilt threads.

37 The top view of an early embroidered pincushion (p. 8) worked in Satin stitch with silk thread on satin over a twill foundation. The button is covered with gold brocade and all edges are finished with twist cord

Sequins

Coloured metal sequins in all shapes and sizes are used on embroidered tops, with or without beads, or as the only decoration. Nearly all are drilled with small holes for sewing; those with the larger holes can be pinstuck also. Sources of supply are the same as for beads and bugles.

38 *left* Sequins of various shapes
right Assorted round sequins

Shells

Shell decoration usually is applied to whatever kind of container holds the pincushion, but shells from necklaces, which are already drilled for threading, can be sewn to the top cover on the edges, where they will not interfere with the pins.

Sea-shore shells can be collected in quantity from the beaches, some of which are famous for them, notably in Dorset, Cornwall and Devon, and on the North-East coast of England. They can be collected often from jumble sales and similar sources.

39 An assortment of shells (limpets, cockles, mussels, scallops, whelks, elephant tusks, cowries) collected from beaches with (*below, centre*) small snail shells which came from necklaces, and are drilled

Other decorations

Many kinds of decoration, other than embroidery, have been lavished or inflicted on pincushions. In addition to the 'hardware' of shells, beads, bugles and the pins themselves, lace, cords, ric-rac and other braids, bobble, tassel and other fringes are commonplace.

Beads and bugles are used with or without other embroidery, and are attached to the top cover by sewing, or with pins. They can be expensive to buy and not always easy to find in shops outside London, but market stalls and second-hand shops often have bead necklaces and dress trimmings, which are cheap. Jumble sales are also a source of supply and beads can be found there in old tobacco tins, pill-boxes and aspirin bottles.

Bugles and small beads are sewn on singly, or threaded and stitched into patterns, fringes and tassels. Large beads with holes large enough to take a pin, are used for pinstuck patterns, or for pinstuck feet on pinballs.

Sewing needles (sharps) sizes 9 to 13 will take most beads, and special beading needles usually are less useful for the sewing.

Fine thread to match the needle is needed. Silk will do for sewing single beads, but cotton should be used for threading and if it can be waxed, so much the better. Candle wax can be used by drawing the thread over a candle or by using an old thread-waxer, often owned but not recognised for what it is.

White or yellow brass lace pins are the most suitable for decoration, as they will not corrode for a very long time.

40 A Tonbridge Ware pincushion and thread waxer

41 An assortment of beads and bugles bought in an old 'Three Nuns' tobacco box, after washing, sorting and threading
top left Coloured 'pearls', 'amethysts', 'rubies' and jet
top right Small coloured glass & metal beads for threading
middle left Wooden beads for pinstuck feet
bottom left Jet and gold-coloured bugles
bottom right Gold-coloured and metal beads for threading and pinsticking

Stitches

Almost every stitch ever known to embroidery has been used in making pincushions, and details for working those most used in illustrated examples are given.

Back stitch

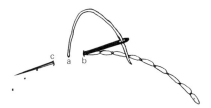

42 Back stitch

This stitch is intended to make a single unbroken line in a pattern and sometimes is the basic for, and used with, other embroidery stitches. (See Pekinese stitch p. 37.)

Bringing out the thread at *a*, the needle is inserted at *b* (the place of exit of the previous stitch), and brought out again at *c*; the distance between the points should be equal.

Double back stitch

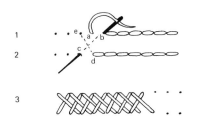

43 Double back stitch

In this stitch two parallel lines of back stitch are worked simultaneously, by making a stitch alternately on each of two rows.

1   After making a back stitch on the top row, from *a* to *b*, the needle crosses under the material, coming out at *c* in the lower row, and to the left of the previous stitch, at point *d*.

2   The needle is then inserted at point *d*, coming out at *e* in the top row; the next stitch is made by returning to *a*, and coming out at *e* again.

3   The process is repeated again as long as necessary.

Blanket stitch

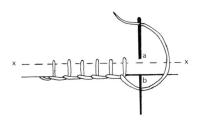

44 Blanket stitch

This is a practical and decorative stitch used as an edging or means of joining pincushion tops and sides (Fig. 71), as well as a surface embroidery. (Figs. 71, 119.) The stitches can be spaced singly or in groups. When used as an edging, a single-turn hem tacked on the wrong side is sufficient; using the line of tacking as a guide, the blanket stitching is worked over it on the right side, taking in the hem at the same time.

The thread should be started on the back of the hem by making a back stitch. Bringing the thread under the hem to the right side, and, holding down the loop, the needle is inserted at point *a*, just over the line of tacking (marked *x*), and bringing it out under the hem again, through the loop at *b*, before drawing the thread through. This is repeated, with evenly spaced stitches until the hem is complete.

Blanket stitch join

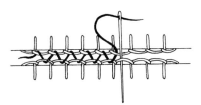

45 Blanket stitch join

Blanket stitched edges make a serviceable join when a thread of self-coloured or contrasting thread is laced through the loops at the edge. This is done by passing the thread under and over the loops on alternate sides, and drawing the edges together as the work proceeds.

Bullion stitch

Bullion stitch can be used either as a decorative stitch or, especially in pincushions, as a means of joining two sides of an outer cover. (Figs. 62, 114, 129.) Technically it is not difficult but a little experience to get the knack of it will improve the final result.

1   The thread is brought out at point *a*, and the needle inserted at *b*, coming out again at *a*, but without pulling the needle right through.

2   The thread is then wound round the needle as often as needed, according to the length of the finished stitch.

3   The thread should be coiled closely, and while holding down the coils, the needle should be drawn carefully through from *b* to *a* and through the coils, until they are transferred to the thread. This should be pulled firmly enough to compress them. The needle is then inserted again at point *b*, drawing the thread through, until the coil lies flat.

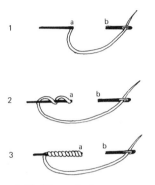

46 Bullion stitch

Buttonhole stitch

A simple Buttonhole loop has been as much a basic stitch of domestic sewing as hemming and running, and it is not surprising that it is used so much in pincushion making, where it is common as a means of joining seams and making buttons and button loops. (Figs. 64, 65, 124.) For whichever purpose, the loops must be sturdy enough to hold a seam or fastening, and a suitable thread, such as buttonhole twist or linen, is advisable.

1   For each loop, a foundation stitch is made by bringing up the thread at a point on the material, *a*, inserting the needle at point *b*, and coming out again at *c*, the intervening distance between *a* and *b*, depending on the purpose of the loop. (For a button loop, the thread required to go over the button should be tried, and if needed for a laced join, the size of the cord and tassel.) From *c*, a series of loops as for Blanket stitch are made over the foundation stitch, until point *d* is reached. For the next loop, and at a distance equal to that between *a* and

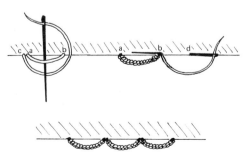

47 Buttonhole stitch

b, the needle is inserted at *d* and the process as for the first loop, repeated as often as necessary.

2   A series of loops for a seam join. Lacing the loops is the same process as for Blanket stitched edges on Figure 45.

Chevron stitch

Chevron stitch is used on a number of pincushions, as an outline and a border pattern, as well as in conjunction with other stitches, especially those by the counted thread. (Fig. 83.) It must be worked with accuracy and precision, so working by the counted thread can be an advantage. The complete pattern is worked in two parallel rows and although the diagram stitches are shown larger than usual, on Fig. 48, the stitches are worked over two threads; there is no rule of thumb which applies.

1   To begin, the thread is brought out on the lower row at *a*, and counting four threads to the right, the needle is inserted at *b*, and brought out at *c*, exactly at the middle of the first stitch. For subsequent stitches on the diagram, the procedure is shown from *c*, in the middle of the second stitch on the lower row. So, counting four threads up from *c*, the needle is inserted at *d*, and brought out two threads to the left at *e*. Then counting four threads to the right, the needle is inserted at *f* and back again to *d*.

2   Counting four threads down from *d*, and two to the right, the needle is inserted at *g*, coming out two threads to the left at *h*.

3   Next, counting four threads to the right, the needle is inserted at *j* and brought back again to *g*, in position to repeat the sequence as from *c*.

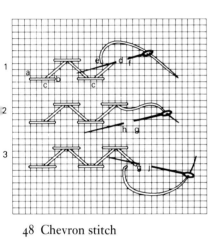

48 Chevron stitch

Coral stitch

This stitch is more easily worked over a marked outline (by pencil or transfer), and the material turned as the work proceeds, so that the line of stitches is made always from right to left.

1   The thread is brought up at X in the first place and a series of looped knots are made at regular intervals.

2   To make each knot, the thread is brought out as at point *a*. Holding down the thread below the marked line, the needle is inserted at point *b*, carrying the thread under *c* and over the loop at *d*, and then pulled firmly to make a knot.

The spacing of the knots can be varied to suit the pattern, or according to the thickness of the embroidery thread.

49 Coral stitch

31

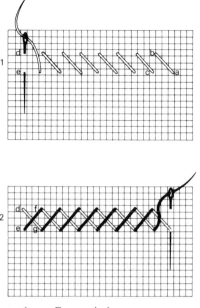

Cross stitch

This stitch can be worked by the counted thread on evenly woven materials, such as linen or canvas, or with the guidance of smocking transfer dots. The stitch is made by working twice over the same ground in opposite directions.

1   Bringing up the needle at point *a*, and then counting three threads to the left and three threads up, it is inserted at point *b*, and brought out again at *c*. This is repeated, working from right to left, to the end of the row, making slanting stitches three threads apart. The number of threads between each stitch can vary, according to the thickness of embroidery thread and coarseness of the material.

2   At the end of the first row, with a stitch made through points *d* and *e*, the needle is next inserted at point *f* and brought out again at point *g*. Then using the same holes as for the first row but working from left to right, the second row is continued to the starting place of the first row.

50 & 51 Cross stitch

Darning stitch

As an overall background stitch, this is a useful one for pincushion tops. It is an advantage to work it by the counted thread on linen, as the lines of stitches should be kept straight, and, when used for pincushions, the stitches should be short. The pattern on Fig. 86, was worked in natural linen thread, but in many cases a fairly dark colour on a light ground is more practical and often enhances the pattern, especially when the outlines are worked in double running.

The stitch is made by picking up one thread of material between evenly spaced surface stitches, which cover two, three or four threads, or whatever suits the work. Each row of stitches should be close to, but not touching its neighbour.

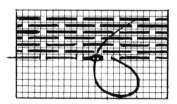

52 Darning stitch

Diamond filling stitch

This stitch is worked in two alternate parallel rows at a time, in the manner of Double Back stitch, and can be worked over two or three threads of the material. The diagram shows the pattern worked over two threads, which are counted throughout.

1   To begin, the needle is brought up at point *a*, and counting two threads to the right, is inserted at *b*, coming out again two threads down and two to the left at *c*.

2   Then, counting two threads to the right, the needle is inserted at *d*, coming out one thread up and four to the left, at *e*.

3 From point *e*, counting two threads to the right, the needle is inserted at *f*, coming out again at *g*, two threads to the left and two down.

4 When sufficient pairs of stitches have been made for the downward direction, the needle is inserted two threads to the left of the last exit, and coming out one thread up and four to the left, continuing as before, but working the rows in an upward direction, as in diagram 5.

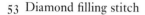

53 Diamond filling stitch

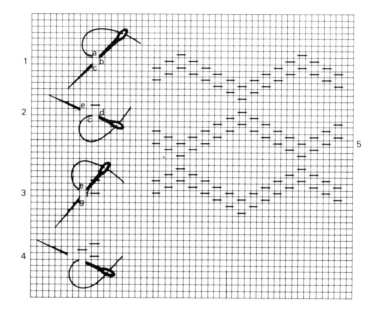

Double faggot stitch

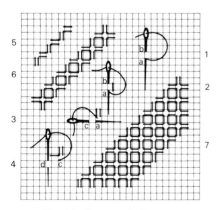

54 Double faggot stitch

This pattern depends for its effect on the thread being pulled firmly after each stitch, which is made by the counted thread. It is worked in diagonal lines and always in the same direction, from right to left for a right-handed worker and left to right for the left-handed.

1 The thread is brought out at point *a*, and the needle inserted two threads above at *b*, coming out again at *a*.

2 Stitch no. 1 is repeated in the same holes.

3 The needle is inserted two threads to the left at point *c*, coming out again at *a*.

4 Inserting the needle again at *c*, it is brought out again two threads down at *d*, and the pattern repeated as from diagram 1.

5 The first row completed.

6 The second row completed.

7 A section of the stitch used as filling. (See the corners of the Wrist Cushion on Fig. 106.)

33

Double running

On the surface this stitch resembles Back stitch, but living up to its name, it is made by running twice over the same track, so that the pattern is the same on the back as on the front. This skill is somewhat lost on a pincushion top unless it is a removable cover. Evenness of stitching is very necessary and is easier of achievement if the work is done on linen, or a material in which the threads can be counted. The diagrams show the working in large scale, of part of the central pattern of Fig. 83.

1   Bringing up the thread at *a*, the needle is inserted, three threads to the right in an upward diagonal direction at *b*, and brought out again at *c*, the needle is then inserted at *d*, and the pattern so continued round its outline.

2   For clarity, the second running stitches are shown black, although the same thread is used throughout, whatever the colour. The second journey is begun by bringing up the thread at *b*, inserting the needle at *c* and coming out again at *d*, and so covering the spaces left in the first journey. Single stitches, such as the points in Figs. 86, 137, can be worked on the first or second round, by making a single stitch (like a Back stitch), returning to its starting point.

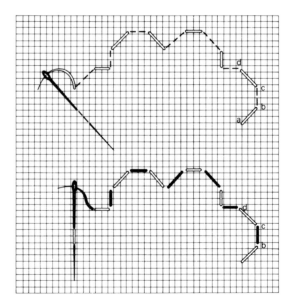

55 Double running stitch

Eyelet

This stitch is used many times in pincushion patterns, usually singly. It is worked by the counted thread, and the stitches pulled firmly, all emerging through a single point of exit, so that it is enlarged into a noticeable hole. The stitch can be used on linen or fine canvas, and worked with silk, linen or wool thread. It seems often to create a focal point in the pattern of the small area of a pincushion top, dominating one (Plate opp. p. 73), giving character to another (Fig. 129), or sometimes in variation making a border pattern for others. (Fig. 124.)

The outline of each unit should be square, and to maintain this shape, the stitches must be worked over a uniform number of threads. There should be sixteen stitches only for each eyelet, radiating like spokes from the centre, with a longer stitch at the corners.

The thread should be brought up at the designated centre point, and working over the surrounding threads, the needle is inserted on the outer edge, and brought up in the original centre point, the thread being drawn firmly. This is repeated, moving on one thread with each stitch, until the eye has sixteen lashes. Care should be taken to keep an even tension, so that the eye is rounded and open.

56 Eyelet

Fishbone stitch

This is used generally as a filling for various shapes, as it is possible to lengthen or shorten the individual stitches to fit almost any pattern outline. The name is descriptive, as a central line is always maintained in the pattern whatever the outline, and the result much like a fish backbone with a spine. As a geometrical pattern it was used in the centre and corners of Fig. 129. The slant of the stitches can be adapted to suit a pattern, although always kept parallel throughout, and although a linen thread was used on Fig. 129, silk also can be used.

In order to maintain a straight 'spine', a line of running stitches with fine thread is made down the centre of the pattern, and each of the embroidery stitches is worked over it in turn.

Beginning at the top, the thread is brought out on the outer edge of one side at *a*, and a slanting stitch made, inserting the needle at *b* (just covering the centre running stitch line), and coming out at *c*, on the opposite outline.

The next stitch is made in the reverse direction; from *c* the thread is taken to a point just below *b*, the needle going in just over the line of running, over-lapping the first stitch slightly and coming out again just below *a*. The process is repeated until the pattern is complete.

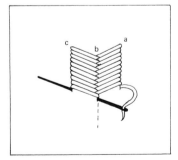

57 Fishbone stitch

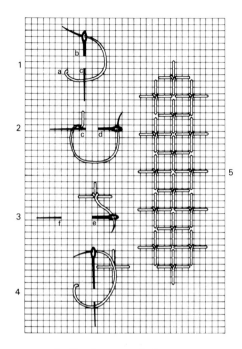

58 Greek cross stitch

Greek cross stitch

The diagrams show the stitch worked over three threads but the fineness of the linen and the general effect needed, should be considered. As with Double Faggot stitch, the thread should be pulled firmly after each stitch and the stitches worked diagonally in rows. The stitch is used generally as a filling.

1 The thread is brought out at point *a*, and is held down as for blanket stitch (p. 29) while three threads are counted to the right and three threads up, to point *b*. The needle is then inserted at *b*, coming out again three threads lower at *c*.

2 Counting three threads to the right of *c*, a stitch is made from *d* back to *c*.

3 To complete one cross, three threads are counted from *c* to *e*, and six to the left from *e* to *f*, and a stitch made from *e* to *f*.

4 Repeat here from diagram 1, until the required amount of ground is covered.

Open window stitch

This is a variation of the Window stitch (p. 39). With a wider spacing of two unworked threads between the stitches and rows, and with the pulling of the stitches, a more open 'window' is made.

1 Bringing out the needle at *a*, a stitch is made by inserting it two threads to the right and three threads lower, at point *b*, and coming out again six threads to the left, at *c*.

2 Counting two threads to the right of *c*, and three threads up to *d*, a stitch is made from *d* to *e*, six threads to the left.

3 Counting two threads to the right and three threads down from *e*, the needle is inserted at *f*, coming out again six threads to the left at *g*.

4 When the row is completed, the work is turned upside down for the return row, leaving two threads unworked between the rows.

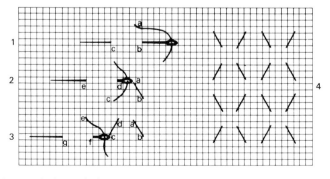

59 Open window stitch

Pekinese stitch

This is an elaboration of Back stitch (p. 29) and is useful and good wearing, as it is closely worked and firm. It is used frequently as a decorative outline to other patterns, as on Fig. 106, and often worked in two colours.

1 The basis of the stitch is a single line of Back stitch.

2 After the Back stitch is completed, another thread is inserted behind each stitch, but without taking up any material. Some workers prefer to insert the threaded eye of the needle instead of the point to do the threading, otherwise a blunt crewel needle can be used.

Working from left to right, the thread is brought up at point *d*, just below the Back stitch line, and inserted two stitches ahead, drawing the thread through, while holding down the loop with the thumb. Inserting the needle again one stitch back, and coming out over the loop of thread (as in Blanket stitch), the thread is drawn firmly through. The finished stitch should be more closely drawn than shown in the diagram.

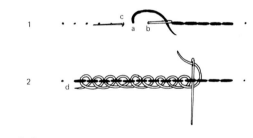

60 Pekinese stitch

Satin stitch

Satin stitch is aptly named, as the result should be of a smooth surface, with even, closely worked stitches covering the pattern from edge to edge. It is popular for pincushion patterns.

The diagram shows the pattern partly worked on a leaf pattern, with the needle being inserted on the outside edge at point *b*, with the thread having been carried over from point *a*. Working in evenly parallel lines, each subsequent stitch is made by inserting the needle at a point (*b*) exactly opposite to the point of exit of the previous stitch (*a*) and returning under the material, near to, but not crowding, point *a*. The process is repeated until the ground is covered, the length of each stitch being governed by the space within the outlines.

The stitch can be useful for geometrical patterns, worked over one, two or three threads, which can be seen on Figs. 83 and 102.

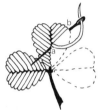

61 Satin stitch

Wave stitch

This stitch, with Window and Open Window stitches (pp. 36, 39) are all similar and often used as fillings or background patterns on pincushion tops, as they are simple to make and suffer little damage in use. Wave stitch is a comparatively close stitch and suitable for finer threads and materials, and the other two for rather coarser ones. In all three the thread is pulled firmly after each stitch.

1　To begin, the thread is brought out at point *a*, and after counting two threads to the right and four down, the needle is inserted at *b*, coming out again at *c*, four threads to the left.

2　Entering again at *a*, a stitch is made by counting four threads to the left and coming out at *d*.

3　The thread is now in position to repeat the pattern to the end of the required row. (See 4 on the diagram.) When the end is reached, it should be brought out eight threads down, ready for the return row.

4　The first row of v patterns reversed.

5　For the return row, the work should be turned upside down, and the pattern repeated as from 1 to 4, and with succeeding rows until the filling is completed.

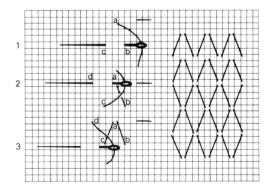

62 Wave stitch

Window stitch

This stitch is used a good deal on pincushion tops and looks much the same as Wave stitch, except that one unworked thread is left between each unit of the pattern and between each row, so that more space (a 'window') is left between the stitches.

1   To begin, the thread is brought out at *a*, and counting two threads to the right and four down, the needle is inserted at *b*, coming out again five stitches to the left at *c*.

2   Next, inserted at *d* (one thread to the left of *a*), and counting five threads to the left of *d*, the needle is brought out at *e*. Re-entering at one thread to the left of *c*, the sequence is continued to the end of the required row. To be in position for the return row, the needle is inserted one thread to the left of the last *c* position and brought out again five threads *below*.

3   Turning the material upside down, the process is repeated in both directions, until the ground is covered. The diagram shows three repeats.

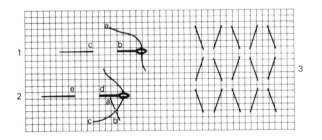

63 Window stitch

Buttons, tassels and cords

The dorset wheel button

Materials
Small bone, plastic or metal ring.
Silk, cotton linen or wool thread, to match the pincushion.

To make a button
1   Tying one end of the thread to the ring, blanket stitch is worked closely over the ring, covering it completely. Without ending off the thread, the stitches are turned over the ring, until the loops are on the inside.
2   Still without cutting the thread, it is then wound over at regular intervals from edge to edge, to form the 'spokes'. The number varies according to the diameter of the button: six will do for a small button. The diagram with twelve spokes is suitable for a one inch (2.5 cm) diameter button. The thread may be finished off here.
3   The point at which the spokes cross in the centre should be stitched across, to draw them together evenly. (See 2.) Then after fastening a thread securely at the back of this point, it should be brought up between two spokes to the front, and a back stitch made over and under the spoke on the right, under the spoke on the left and brought up in position for the stitch to be repeated, all round the wheel.
4   The process is continued, over one spoke and under two, until the middle of the button is filled.

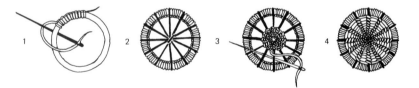

64 The Dorset Wheel button

Round stuffed button

Materials
Soft padding, such as cotton wool, sheep's wool, unravelled fine knitting etc. wound into a small ball.
Thread for stitching can be silk, cotton, linen or wool, whichever has been used for the pincushion. (Fig. 129.)

To make the button
1   The padding should be wound or rolled to the required size and for ease in handling, this may be done round a smooth matchstick or a blunt-ended needle or threader.
2   The round pad is then embroidered all over with blanket stitch. Beginning at the top a stitch is made in the centre and working in anti-

clockwise direction a circle of blanket stitching is made. A second round is made by working into each stitch of the row above, taking in a little of the padding as well, and spacing each a little wider to allow for the increase in girth of the button, until half way down. After this the spacing gradually narrows until the bottom centre point is reached.

3 The blanket stitching should cover the padding completely; the diagram shows the work enlarged. To finish the button, the stick or needle should be removed and a looped shank made by the method shown for button loops on p. 30.

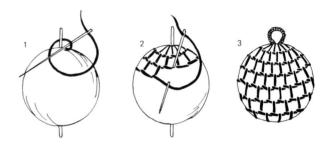

65 Round stuffed button

Bar button or tassel

Materials
Thread: silk, cotton, linen or wool. If good quality linen has been used for the pincushion, left-over pieces can be unravelled and used for the core of a button.
Thin card or very stiff paper.

To make the button
1 Cut two pieces of thin card, a little wider than the finished length of the button. Holding them together, the thread for the core of the button is wound over; this should be done smoothly, with the threads close but not over lapping. When sufficient has been wound, scissors should be slid between the cards and the wound threads cut through on both sides from *a* to *b* and *c* to *d*.

2 Holding the cut threads in a bundle, and beginning a short way from the end, the binding thread should be fastened by making a stitch through the bundle, and then wound smoothly and finished off a short way from the other end, to make the bar.

3 The uneven ends of the core should be trimmed neatly and 'roughed up' a little to make a short tufted end. A shank of matching thread made as a button loop (p. 30) should be sewn on the side. When used as a tassel, the binding thread can be the same as that used for the cord. (Fig. 137.)

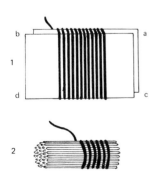

66 Bar button or tassel

A simple tassel

Materials
Thread: Silk, cotton, linen or wool.
Card: Two pieces, the width to be that of the length of tassel.

To make a tassel
1 Holding together the cards, the thread should be wound over, closely but not overlapping; the amount wound depends on whether a fat or slim tassel is needed.
2 Before removing the cards, a threaded needle should be run between them at the top. Scissors should then be slid between them at the lower edge and the threads cut through. Holding them firmly, the threads are then gathered up, and the tassel tied at the top.
3 A thread is then wound round the tassel to make a head, and the threads at the bottom trimmed to make a tidy finish.

  Decoration can be added to the head; Blanket stitch, as on the round button, can be used; the binding can be done with a fine plait or cord; the tassel threads can be of mixed or selected colours or the binding can be of a different colour, and so on. (Figs. 77, 101, 124, 132, 137.)
4 An even simpler finish for a tassel is to gather the threads as in Fig. 2, and, still attached to the gathering thread, draw them into one end of a bead. The size of the hole in the bead will limit the number of threads, but this is a useful method for small tassels of silk or stranded cotton.

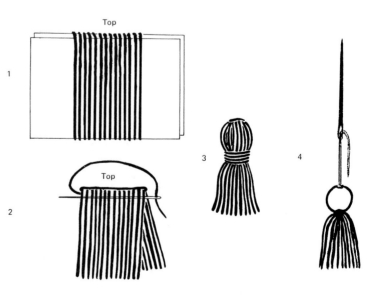

67 A simple tassel

Bead tassels

This kind of tassel is quick and simple to make and can be used to finish up an assorted lot of beads. Any size can be used, and several sizes be put into one tassel.

1   A looped tassel is made by stringing a number of beads, and picking up the thread between beads at regular intervals and sewing it to the point at which the tassel is needed.

The beads at the bottom of each loop are sometimes larger or of a different colour.

2, 3   Other looped tassels can be made by stringing shorter lengths of double that needed for the tassel, and passing the thread for each loop through a large bead, making a stitch on the cushion and returning through the bead head to collect another string.

4   Single thread tassels are made by taking the thread through a bead head as before, threading the required number of beads, but ending with a larger bead and a small one, and then (5) returning through the larger bead and the string and the bead head, and sewing to the cushion.

6   This is repeated for each string of the tassel.

68 Bead tassels

A simple twist cord

A simple cord can be made by twisting together a number of threads, using those to match the cotton or silk embroidery on the pincushion. A skein of silk or stranded cotton is very suitable. The length of cord needed should be measured, whether for fastening (124, 137), hanging (147), or finishing (173), and the length of thread required to make the cord, should be three times this amount – for 12 inches of cord (30 cm), 36 inches (90 cm) of thread will be needed, and so on. The colours can be mixed to make a mottled cord, or in selected or self colours, to suit the work.

To make the cord
Knot together one end of the threads, and fix them to something firm. For a small fine cord, a weighted or fixed pincushion is adequate.

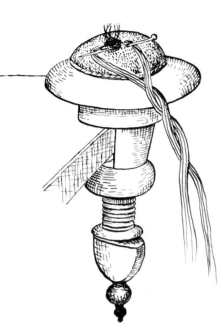

Holding the other end and keeping the threads firmly stretched, they should be twisted in one direction until they will not twist any more.

To finish
Still holding the ends firmly stretched with one hand, and the exact centre of the twist with the finger and thumb of the other, it should be folded over from this point, until both ends can be held together. The centre is then released, and the folded twist will then twist itself into a firm cord.

When the knot is undone, the ends can be sewn into a tassel finish, (Fig. 67) or tucked into a small opening between the edges of the pincushion cover, and sewn firmly.

69a Twisted cord

69b The finished twistcord

A three-fold plait

A plait has been a usual means of suspending pincushions which have been worn hanging from a waist-belt, such as the pin-balls (147), hand-made sewing companions, or some of the late 19th century parlour pincushions, intended to hang on the wall, in place of ribbon or cord.

As with the twisted cord, a plait can be made of threads to match those used for the pincushion; in the case of knitted pin-balls (p. 80) silk knitting thread was used and for the companion, silk thread or stranded cotton (p. 66).

A number of threads are used for each fold of the plait, depending on the required thickness. When light and dark colours are combined, it has been usual to use one fold of the dark, and two of the light colours.

70 Three-fold plait

Box and mattress pincushions

Rectangular box pincushion

A box pincushion, covered with pink and grey art felt, embroidered with Blanket stitch and couching in white, grey and pink silk. Base and sides are stiffened, and filled with wool. ($3 \times 4\frac{1}{2} \times 1\frac{1}{2}$ inches), ($8 \times 11 \times 4$ cm).

Materials
Art felt. About 10×10 inches (25×25 cm). Calico or sateen, about 12×12 inches (30×30 cm). Transfer no. FS 113 (p. 120).
Thread: silks, silk twist, or stranded cotton.
Medium stiff card. Sheep's wool or unravelled wool.

To make the box
Five pieces of card should be cut, one measuring $4\frac{1}{2} \times 3$ inches (11×8 cm) for the base; two pieces measuring $4\frac{1}{2} \times 1\frac{1}{2}$ inches (11×4 cm) for the sides; and two pieces measuring $3 \times 1\frac{1}{2}$ inches (8×4 cm) for the ends.

71 Rectangular box pincushion

Each card is covered separately with calico or sateen, cut to give ample turnings all round. The turnings are held with long stitches from side to side and a back stitch on each corner fold.

The covered pieces are joined by oversewing the calico at the ends of each and drawing them firmly together. They are then sewn by the same method to the base, resulting in a lid-less box.

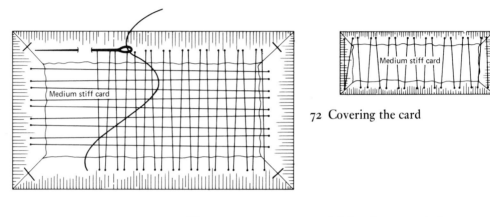

72 Covering the card

73 Joining the covered pieces

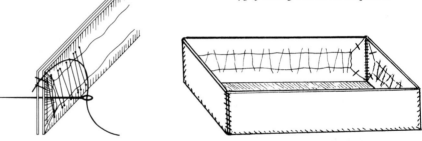

To make the outer cover

The transfer should be applied on to the felt and the patterns embroidered before the pieces are cut out. Appropriate turnings for each piece are allowed on the transfer.

The patterns are worked in Blanket stitch with some couched lines of silk twist.

With the embroidery completed, the sections should be cut out and turnings made and tacked on the wrong side, taking care not to stretch the felt. All the edges should then be worked over with Blanket stitch on the right side (Fig. 75). Make sure that the stitches take in the turnings at the back as the tackings are removed after making up.

75 (Wrong side of felt) Blanket stitches cover the turning

74 Couched lines of silk twist

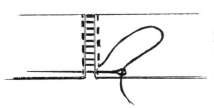

76 Joining the edges of the long strip

The long strip for the sides should be fitted round the side pieces and joined in the middle of one end by sewing with plain ladder stitch and drawn together until the edges meet (Fig. 76).

All the cover pieces are joined by sewing through the loops of the Blanket stitches (p. 29) and the stuffing inserted just before the 'lid' is finally joined.

Square box pincushion

The cover of linen is embroidered in cross, satin and double running stitches with silks in shades of red, pink, brown, green and yellow. Corner tassels are made of mixed silks used for the embroidery. The pad is of thick wool felt measuring $3\frac{1}{4} \times 3\frac{1}{4} \times \frac{3}{4}$ inches ($8.2 \times 8.2 \times 2$ cm).

Materials
Natural linen. About 8×8 inches (20×20 cm).
Thread: Silk or stranded cotton. Tacking thread.
Filling: Thick wool felt for one or more layers.

77 Square box pincushion

To mark the cover
The linen should be marked out, the marking done with pencil and the lines covered with tackings as a permanent guide; turnings allowances should be made also.

To make the pad
One or more pieces of thick felt or woollen fabric should be cut to shape, $3\frac{1}{4} \times 3\frac{1}{4}$ inches (8.2×8.2 cm), until the thickness is $\frac{1}{4}$ inch or 2 cm. Two or more pieces should be stitched together.

To make the tassels
These are simple tassels with Blanket stitch heads, made as in the diagrams on p. 42.

To make the cover
The embroidery should be worked before cutting out the pieces. One quarter of the top is shown (Fig. 79), and the whole of one side (Fig. 80). There is no pattern on the base, but the edges are Satin stitched.

With the embroidery completed, the pieces should be cut out and turnings made and tacked on the wrong side.

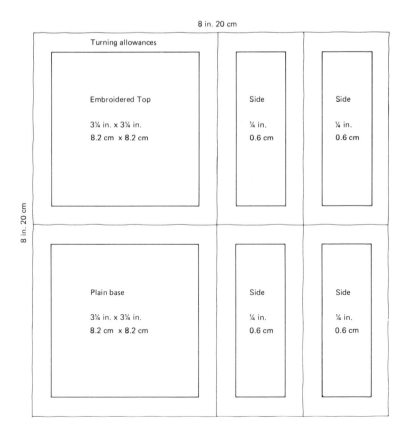

78 The linen marked out before cutting

Twentieth century sewing companion, a sewing companion mounted in an example of contemporary craftsmanship in Battersea enamel with gilt mounts. The thimble is held on a gilt fitting in the middle of a pink velvet cushion, which is attached by adhesive in the container. The height of the container is 2½ inches (6.5cm) and the circumference of the pincushion is 7½ inches (9cm)

A nineteenth century bead embroidered hanging pincushion.
The foundation is red velvet, embroidered with clear glass and opaque beads, and
finished with a fringe and tassels of beads. Two twisted strings of white glass beads on
strong white thread are used to hang the cushion. The cushion has been well used,
as most of the pile has worn off the velvet

A selection of embroidered and bead-stuck pincushions

Top   *Round pillow type of cushion covered with quilted silk. The top pattern is worked with cord and the sides with flat quilting. The reverse side is made of wadded quilting*

Left   *A box cushion, the cover worked with wool on canvas*

Right   *Mattress cushion made of linen worked in patterns of pulled stitches*

The edges are joined on the right side by sewing, with a matching thread, through the Satin stitching.

The pad should be put into the cover before the last side is sewn on. When all the joins are completed, the tassels should be sewn on to the four top corners.

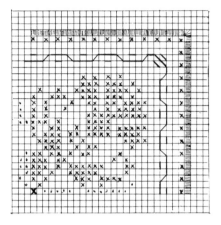

79 Embroidery guide for top

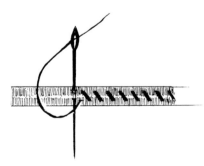

80 Embroidery guide for side

81 Joining the edges

82 A small hexagonal pincushion made of patchwork

Another square box pincushion

The cover is of fine cream linen, embroidered with cream and natural linen thread. Satin and Darning stitches are worked with cream, and Double running and Chevron stitches with natural thread. Design adapted from a 17th century sampler. Signed and dated in blue silk thread ETTA CAMPBELL TWYFORD WINCHESTER 1965.

Filling, a woollen pad. $3\frac{1}{2} \times 3\frac{1}{2} \times \frac{1}{2}$ inches ($9 \times 9 \times 1.5$ cm).

Materials
Fine evenweave linen, about 8×10 inches (20×25 cm).
Thread: Fine cream and natural linen thread, tacking cotton.
Layers of woollen fabric.

To mark the cover
The section for top and sides is made in one piece and the linen so marked, defining the corner squares, which are not embroidered. The base is made separately; all sections should be marked with turning allowances.

To make the cover
The top and base are worked with different patterns, except for the Chevron stitch borders.

All stitches are worked by the counted thread, taking up two threads at a time.

83 Square box pincushion

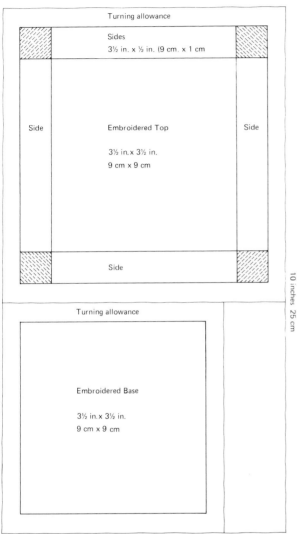

84 The marked cover

Within the diagram (figure 84):

Turning allowance

Sides
3½ in. x ½ in. (9 cm. x 1 cm

Side · Embroidered Top · Side

3½ in. x 3½ in.
9 cm x 9 cm

Side

Turning allowance

Embroidered Base

3½ in. x 3½ in.
9 cm x 9 cm

10 inches 25 cm

8 inches 20 cm

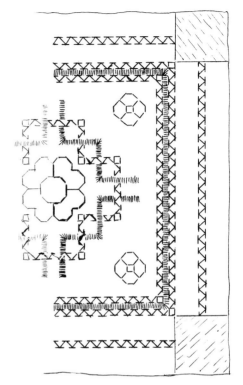

85 Half of the top pattern, with sides

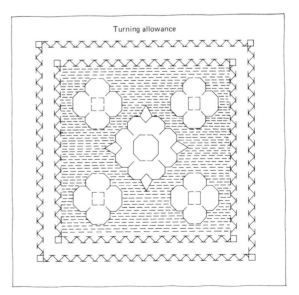

86 The base pattern, with a background of Darning stitch

To make the pad
One or more layers of felt or woollen fabric should be cut to shape ($3\frac{1}{2} \times 3\frac{1}{2}$ inches, 9×9 cm) until the required $\frac{1}{2}$ inch thickness is obtained. More layers than one should be stitched through. (Figs. 30 and 97.)

To make up the cushion
With the embroidery completed, the pieces are cut out and turnings tacked to the wrong side. The piece for the top should be shaped to make the box, by removing a triangular piece for each corner, cutting diagonally from A to B. (Fig. 87.)

A careful cut is then made from the centre of the diagonal at each corner, to just below the border embroidery, from *ab* to *c*.

The triangular 'flaps' thus made are folded back to the wrong side along lines *a* to *c* and *b* to *c*.

The folded edges are then joined by oversewing from *ab* to *c*.

Turning the 'box' right side out, the pad is put in, and the base sewn to the lower edges of the top with oversewing.

To finish the cushion, all the edges are worked over with close Satin stitch, covering completely all the oversewn seams.

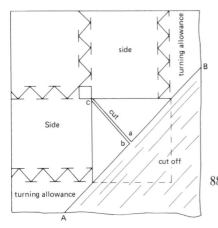

87 Shaping and cutting the top piece

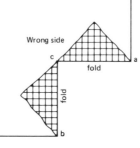

88 Fold back the flaps

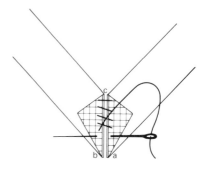

89 Join the folded edges

Mattress pincushion

The sketch is of a red silk mattress cushion, with the edges finished with covered piping cord. The pad is of flannel pieces. $2\frac{1}{2} \times 2 \times \frac{1}{2}$ inches ($5 \times 6.5 \times 1$ cm).

Materials
Strong silk. About 8×8 inches (20×20 cm).
Thread: sewing and tacking cottons. Red buttonhole twist.
Fine piping cord. Flannel or tweed pieces.

To make the pad

Enough flannel pieces should be cut to make a thickness of half an inch when stitched together. The edges should be trimmed to the required size, $2 \times 2\frac{1}{2}$ inches (5×6.5 cm).

To make the cover

Two pieces of silk, each $3 \times 2\frac{1}{2}$ inches (8×6.5 cm) should be cut, and a strip 10×1 inches (25×2.5 cm). Turnings should be made on all edges and tacked to the wrong side.

The piping cord should be covered with matching silk and sewn in with Running stitches (Fig. 91). The silk can be cut on the straight.

The top and base are then joined to the strip by hemming as closely as possible to the piping, putting in the pad before sewing the last side (Fig. 92).

To finish the cushion

Using buttonhole twist and a strong needle, long enough to go through the cushion, it is stitched at evenly spaced intervals from top to base, at least twice at each point, with a Cross or Back stitch. The thread can be taken from one point to another and ended off firmly at the last stitch.

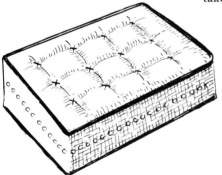

90 Red silk mattress cushion

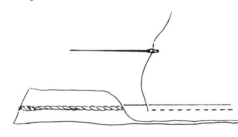

91

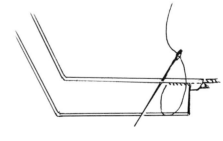

92

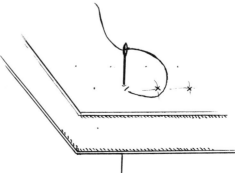

93

Sampler pincushions

Pincushions as small workbox samplers have been made from at least the mid-eighteenth century. During this time, when children were expected to mark the household linen with letters and numerals worked in Cross stitch or 'marking' stitch, their samplers were sometimes made as pincushion covers. More recently, small-scale stitch samplers have been made into pincushions.

Octagonal marking sampler

An eighteenth-century marking sampler, with alphabet and numerals. An inscription on the reverse is 'Hannah Smith.Uttoxeter'. Worked in Cross stitch with black silk on linen. $2\frac{1}{2} \times 2\frac{1}{2} \times \frac{1}{4}$ inches ($6.5 \times 6.5 \times 0.5$ cm).

94 Octagonal marking sampler

Materials
Medium thin card such as postcard.
Linen. About 8×6 inches (20×15 cm). Scraps of flannel or other woollen fabric.
Binding material or tape and narrow silk ribbon, about 12 inches of each. Black embroidery silk. Tacking and sewing cottons.

To make the covers (Fig. 95)
The outlines should be marked on the linen with pencil. (A) An octagonal patchwork template can be used for this.

Inner lines should be marked with a second template, (B) so as to define the areas to be embroidered, (C) and all pencil marks run over with tacking thread to make more permanent guide lines.

The embroidery should be completed before cutting out both pieces along all lines A. (See p. 84 for Alphabets.)

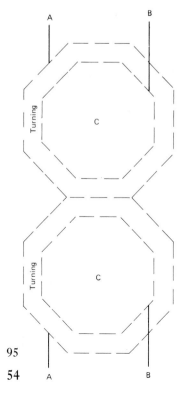

95

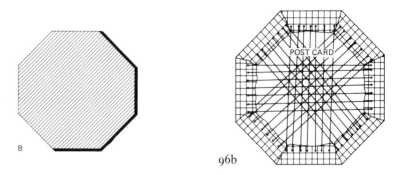

A

B

96a

96b

POST CARD

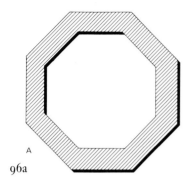

97 Several layers of fabric form the pad

To mount the covers (Fig. 96)
Using template B, two pieces of card should be cut and covered with the embroidered linen pieces, the turning allowance on each being folded over the cards. The turnings are held by sewing them from side to side with a Lacing stitch, making sure that the pattern on the right side is not stretched.

To make the pad (Fig. 97)
A number of woollen fabric pieces should be cut to shape, using template B as a guide, and then stitched together in layers according to the required thickness. The layers should be sewn together with long but tidy stitches, to make a firm pad. Two lines of stitching should be enough.

The pad should be covered at the edges with binding material and Back stitched at the corner folds to keep it firm and tidy (Fig. 98).

Figure 99 shows the finished pad.

To make up the pincushion
The embroidered base and top should be stitched by oversewing to the bound edges of the pad as shown in Fig. 100. Finally a piece of narrow ribbon should be tied round to cover the binding and finished off with a small formal bow on one side. The ribbon can be sewn lightly in place with small running stitches.

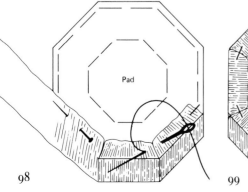

Pad

Pad

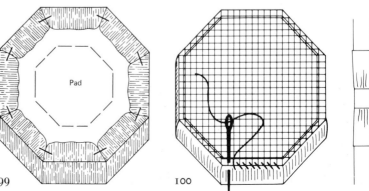

98

99

100

Rectangular sampler pincushion

A late eighteenth- or early nineteenth-century marking sampler, with capitals and miniscule alphabets, and numerals from 1 to 11, worked with pale blue silk on silk gauze. The back of the cover is of pale blue figured silk and the inner cover also is of pale blue silk. Four tassels of cream silk are attached to the corners. $3 \times 1\frac{1}{2}$ inches (8×4 cm).

This small cushion seems never to have been used and possibly was intended only as a marking sampler made in a conventional manner of its time. It is too lightly filled (with a fibrous material, probably wool) for it to have held more than a small pin or two and although no trace remains now, it may also have contained some aromatic powder as a sachet for the workbox.

The filling is in a small bag of blue silk and the outer cover of silk gauze is joined at the edges with fine close Satin stitch in blue silk thread.

The alphabets and numerals (p. 84) are worked over two threads with the same silk, and the cushion is finished with very long simple tassels of cream silk (p. 42).

101 Rectangular sampler pincushion

Hexagonal sampler pincushion

A twentieth-century double-sided sampler pincushion of stitches worked by the counted thread, with natural linen thread on linen. The stitches include Greek cross, Window and Open window, variations of Wave and Satin stitches. Filling is sheep's wool. 3×3 inches (8×8 cm).

Materials
Linen. Natural or coloured. To make 14 one-inch wide (2.5 cm) pieces, giving a finished width of 3 inches (8 cm), about 8×8 inches (20×20 cm) of linen should be allowed. Larger shapes need more material.
Thread: Linen, silk or stranded cotton. Sewing and tacking cottons.
Filling: Sheep's wool or other fibrous material.

To mark the cover (Fig. 103)
Using a hexagonal patchwork template (p. 101) as a guide, mark out 14 sections. Outline A should be marked first; then the inner section C (to be embroidered), is marked with outline B, using a smaller template.

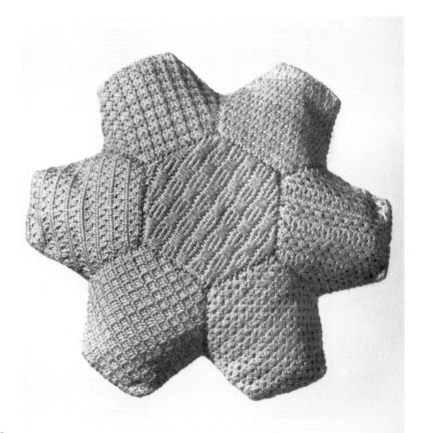

102 Hexagonal sampler pincushion

Pencil can be used for marking, and a tacking thread run over the marks to make a more permanent guide, as the embroidery should be done before the pieces are cut out.

To make the cover
With the embroidery completed in each section, these should be separated by cutting along all lines marked A. The turning allowance on each section should be made and tacked on the wrong side (Fig. 104), and the resulting pieces sewn together by oversewing on the wrong side.

Two groups of seven sections are needed, one group for each side of the pincushion. With the two sides held together, wrong sides outwards, they are joined at the edges by oversewing, but leaving an opening to allow the work to be turned right side out. (Fig. 105.)

After the work has been turned right side out, the filling should be put in, packing it firmly, and the opening neatly joined.

104 Tacking the turning allowance to wrong side

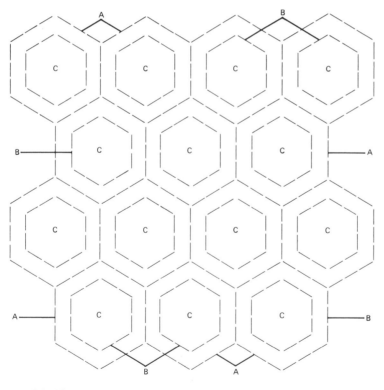

103 Marking out the cover

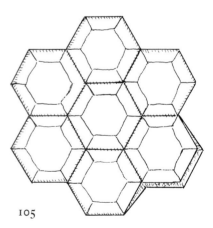

105

58

Dressmaker's pincushions and sewing companions

Dressmaker's wrist pincushion

A box cushion covered with blue linen and embroidered with blue and green silk in Pekinese and Double faggot stitches. The band is removable, made of linen-covered elastic, fastened with hooks and eyes. Filling, sheep's wool. $2 \times 2 \times \frac{3}{4}$ inches ($5 \times 5 \times 2$ cm).

Materials
Evenweave linen: About 10×8 inches (25×20 cm) for the cushion and band. All measurements on the plan (Fig. 107) allow for turnings.
Elastic: About 8 inches (20 cm) of $\frac{1}{2}$ inch (1.5 cm) elastic.
Threads: Coloured silk or stranded cotton. Sewing and tacking cottons. Two hooks and two eyes. Woven or raw wool for filling.

To make the cushion
With the embroidery completed, the pieces should be cut out, and the turnings made and tacked on the wrong side.

The top is shaped by the method used for the box cushion on page 52, but with the corners joined on the wrong side by oversewing, making sure that the embroidered pattern matches on the right side.

106 Dressmaker's wrist pincushion

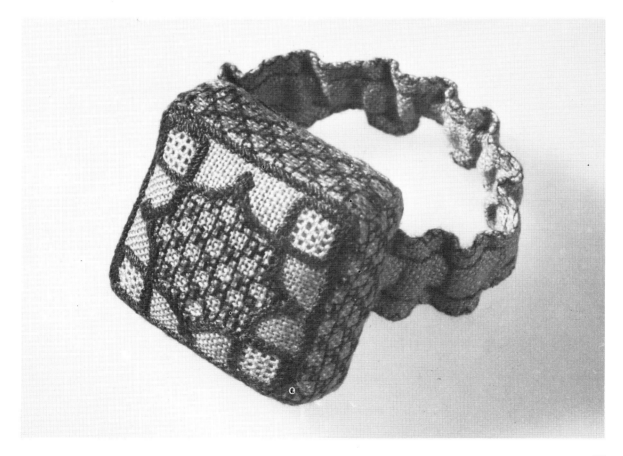

107 Cutting guide

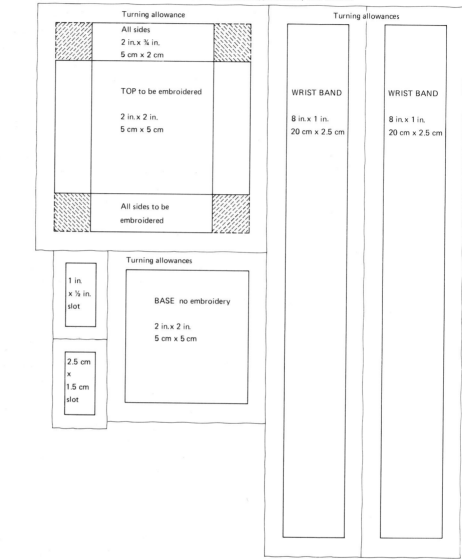

Total measurement approximately 10 x 8 inches

Turning allowance

All sides
2 in. x ¾ in.
5 cm x 2 cm

TOP to be embroidered

2 in. x 2 in.
5 cm x 5 cm

All sides to be
embroidered

1 in.
x ½ in.
slot

2.5 cm
x
1.5 cm
slot

Turning allowances

BASE no embroidery

2 in. x 2 in.
5 cm x 5 cm

Turning allowances

WRIST BAND

8 in. x 1 in.
20 cm x 2.5 cm

WRIST BAND

8 in. x 1 in.
20 cm x 2.5 cm

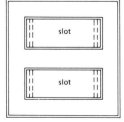

slot

slot

108 Slot pieces (2)

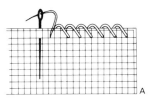

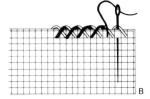

109 Stitching the strips together

Before joining the base to the top and sides, attach the two slot pieces (Fig. 108) to the right side of the base by Back stitching, making sure that they are evenly spaced to take the band, and exactly straight.

The base is attached to the top by oversewing on the wrong side, leaving an opening for the stuffing. The work is then turned inside out, the stuffing put in and the opening neatly joined.

To make the band
Before making up, the width of the band should be checked for fitting through the slots.

Holding the strips, wrong sides together, and using a thread to match the embroidery, the sides only are joined by spaced oversewing at the edges (Fig. 109). This is worked as for Cross stitch, in two directions – from right to left (A) and back again, (B).

To finish the band
Two parallel rows of even running stitches should be made through both thicknesses of material from end to end, the space between them gauged to take the elastic. The elastic is threaded in and the ends secured firmly about half an inch from each end.

To fasten the band (Fig. 110)
Two hooks should be put in at one end by slipping the shanks into the opening, leaving the hooks themselves outside, on the *inner or wrong side* of the band. The hooks are sewn in through the concealed ends of the shank, catching the elastic at the same time. At the other end, but on the *right side* of the band, two buttonholed bars should be made, about a quarter of an inch from the edge, so that when fastened, the hooks are covered and not resting on the wrist.

Finally the ends of the band should be worked with crossed oversewing, as on the sides.

wrong side

right side

110 Band fastenings

Dressmaker's weighted pincushion

A pillow cushion, designed to be used on the padded arm of a chair, or on the knee. The natural linen cover is embroidered with linen thread in a freehand pattern, using Greek cross and Wave fillings, Coral and Satin stitches, with outlines and stems in Back and Double back stitches. The edges are joined with Bullion stitch in pairs, and the weights are covered as for a Dorset button (p. 40). Filling, sheep's wool. $4\frac{1}{2} \times 3\frac{1}{2}$ inches (11×9 cm).

Materials
Evenweave linen: 12×6 inches (30×15 cm) for cover and band allows for turnings. Calico or linen for an under cover.
Threads: Knox's fine linen thread, or embroidery silk or cotton. Sheep's wool. 2 tailor's weights. 2 large beads.

111 Dressmaker's weighted pincushion

To make the cushion

An under cover should be made of linen or calico, measuring $4\frac{1}{4} \times 3\frac{1}{4}$ inches (10.5 × 8.5 cm), leaving one end open. Turning it right side out, the filling should be packed in firmly and the opening neatly sewn together.

The top cover should be embroidered on one piece, then both pieces should be cut out, and turnings made and tacked on the wrong side, each piece measuring $4\frac{1}{2} \times 3\frac{1}{2}$ inches (11 × 9 cm). All the hems are then sewn with Double back stitch on the wrong side, and tacking threads removed.

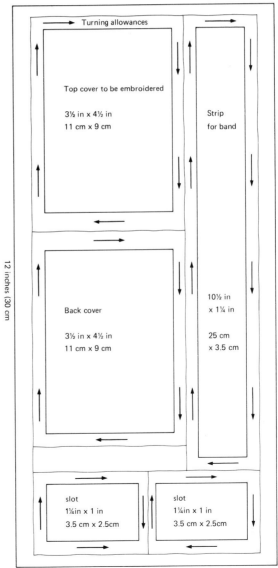

Turning allowances

Top cover to be embroidered

3½ in x 4½ in
11 cm x 9 cm

Strip for band

12 inches (30 cm

Back cover

3½ in x 4½ in
11 cm x 9 cm

10½ in x 1¼ in

25 cm x 3.5 cm

slot
1¼in x 1 in
3.5 cm x 2.5cm

slot
1¼in x 1 in
3.5 cm x 2.5cm

6 inches (15 cm

The two slot pieces should be turned in at the edges and sewn firmly at the ends, to the right side of the cushion base. (Fig. 113.)

Top and base are then joined on the edges with Bullion stitches in pairs, worked on the right side, leaving one end open until the pad is inserted, then completing the joins. (Fig. 114.)

To make the band

The weights and buttons should be covered with linen thread; the weights by the method used for a Dorset button, with 24 spokes on both sides (p. 40). As the weights are solid, the thread must be wound over the edges and worked on both sides. Beginning in the centre two threads at a time are drawn together, but from about half-way towards the edge, the spokes are worked separately (Fig. 115).

The beads are covered by threading through and over with linen thread, until they are covered (Fig. 116).

Turnings should be made on the edges of the band, and the ends folded into points, unwanted material being cut off. The hems are sewn with Double back stitch on the right side (Fig. 117).

The weights are attached by sewing a thread to the point of the band, taking it through the bead, and catching the stitches at the edge of the weight. Then thread back through the bead and finish off firmly at the starting point.

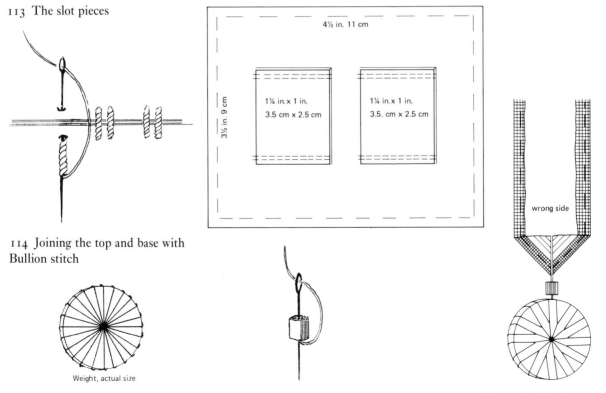

113 The slot pieces

114 Joining the top and base with Bullion stitch

115 Covering the weights

Weight, actual size

116 Covering the beads

117 The end of the bands

4½ in. 11 cm

3½ in. 9 cm

1¼ in. x 1 in.
3.5 cm x 2.5 cm

1¼ in. x 1 in.
3.5. cm x 2.5 cm

wrong side

64

Two brown knitted silk pinballs, 1792 and 1800 (Museum of Costume, Bath)

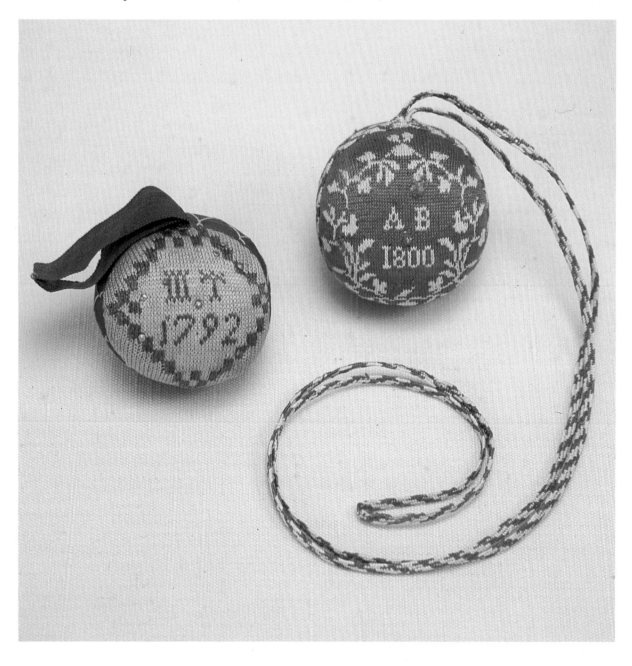

Pincushion decorated with beads and mottoes. Many similar ones were made at the time of the Boer War with the names of the different regiments. They were bought by the soldiers to send home to their sweethearts. Long brass pins, threaded with a variety of beads, hold tinsel threads in position (Collection of Angela Thompson)

Pincushions made from bone, ivory, shells and natural materials. All from the mid nineteenth century (Private collection)

118 A nineteenth-century Dressmaker's Companion. The doll is dressed with a full-skirted silk gown trimmed with pockets intended for small sewing aids such as a thimble, a packet of needles and so on. Pins, and needles when not in use, were kept in the basket-work hat containing a pincushion

119 Embroidered sewing companion

Embroidered sewing companion

A circular pincushion of embroidered felt is included in a hand-made sewing companion (containing also needle, thimble and tape measure cases). The pincushion is made in the same way as the nineteenth century purse and pocket pincushions. The grey felt is embroidered with Blanket stitch and couched braid, with some additional whipping, in black and white. Filling is a small amount of wool or felt. Diameter 3 inches (8 cm).

Materials
Coloured felt: Enough to make two 3½ inch (9 cm) circles; this allows for ¼ inch (0.5 cm) turnings all round.
Ric-rac braid: 18 inches (45 cm) of narrow width.
Embroidery silk or stranded cotton. Tacking cotton.
Thin card: Enough to make two 3 inch (8 cm) circles.
Transfer: No. 108 (this includes the whole 'Companion') p. 120.
Filling: A small amount of wool or felt.

To make the pincushion
The transfer should be ironed on to the felt, with the allowances for turnings, and the embroidery completed before cutting out. The centre patterns, worked in Blanket stitch, can be added to by whipping over with thread of a different colour (Fig. 120).

The braid can be couched on by sewing over once only but is firmer and looks better if a return journey is made in the opposite direction (Fig. 121).

The card circles are then covered, by turning over the felt round the edges on the exact line of the ring of Blanket stitching, and laced across from side to side, taking care not to stretch the felt (Fig. 122).

When covered, the circles should be held with the wrong sides together and a small filling of wool or thin felt put between them. This holds the pins more firmly. The edges are then joined by weaving together the Blanket stitch loops (p. 29).

120 A second colour thread elaborates the Blanket stitch

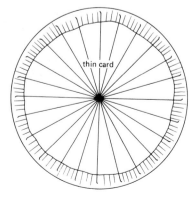
thin card

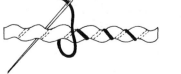

121 Couching the ric-rac braid

122 The covered circles of card

Removable covers

A practical kind of outer cover for many kinds of pincushions is one which can be removed easily for washing or replacement. A number are made of semi-transparent materials, such as muslin or net, or open embroidery or crochet, through which a coloured under cover can be seen. Some are lightly sewn on, others planned to fasten with buttons or ties, others are just pinned on.

Pinned-on top cover

A cover of crochet in linen thread, pinned to a linen box-type of cushion. The pad is of woollen material. $3\frac{3}{4} \times 3\frac{3}{4} \times \frac{3}{4}$ inches ($9.5 \times 9.5 \times 2$ cm).

Materials
Natural or coloured linen: About 9×6 inches (23×15 cm).
Thread: Crochet thread to match. Sewing and tacking cottons.
Pieces of woollen fabric: grey tweed was used for this pad.

To make the cover
The box-shaped cover is made in the same way as on diagram 87, with appropriate measurements. The filling is made of layers of woollen fabric stitched and trimmed to make a pad $3\frac{3}{4} \times 3\frac{3}{4} \times \frac{3}{4}$ inches ($9.5 \times 9.5 \times 2$ cm).

The crochet top can be made from any suitable pattern given in books and magazines on crochet. A square of lace, embroidered net or other embroidery could also be used.

123 Box cushion with removable crochet top

Rectangular bolster cushion

The linen cover is embroidered in Cross stitch, with coloured silks in shades of red, blue, pink and gold colours. The pattern is repeated on the reverse side. The cover is fastened at one end with silk cord and matching silk tassels are attached to the corners. The filling is cedar dust in an under cover. $5\frac{1}{4} \times 2\frac{1}{4}$ inches (13.5×6 cm).

124 Rectangular bolster cushion

Materials
Evenweave linen: About $6\frac{1}{2} \times 6\frac{1}{2}$ inches (17×17 cm). Calico or linen for under cover in the same amount.
Threads: Silk or stranded cotton. Tacking and sewing cottons.
Filling: Cedar dust or fine sawdust.

To make the under cover
To make a well-shaped pad, the material should be cut in two pieces and seamed together, with ample turnings, leaving an opening at one end for filling (Fig. 125).

Turn the cover right side out and fill, sewing the opening.

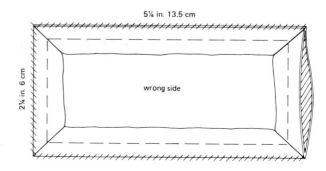

5¼ in. 13.5 cm

2¼ in. 6 cm

wrong side

125 Making the pad

To make the top cover

As the pattern is identical on both sides each can be planned on one piece of linen and marked with turning allowances (Fig. 126). The stitches are worked by the counted thread, over two threads, the diagram (Fig. 127) showing half the plan for one side. The border pattern is a variation of Eyelet stitch (p. 35), worked over four threads.

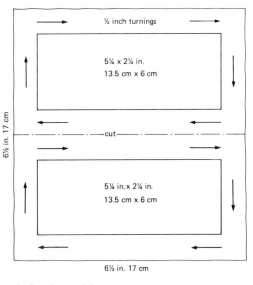

126 Cutting guide

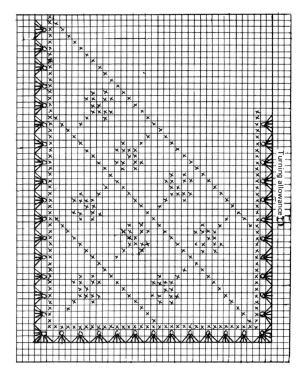

127

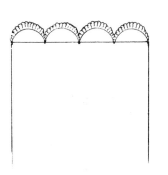

128 Buttonhole loops decorate one end of the bolster

To make up the top cover

With the embroidery completed, turnings on both pieces should be made and tacked on the wrong side.

The pieces are joined on the right side, by turning them with the embroidery facing outwards, and sewing through the loops of the Eyelet stitches on the border. This can be done by lacing together as for Blanket stitch, on diagram 45. Two sides and one end only are joined in this way, the other end being worked with buttonhole loops on both edges (Fig. 128).

The loops should be large enough to take a fine cord, which is threaded through them and tied to fasten.

The cord should be made of silk thread matching that used for the border pattern and buttonhole loops, by the method on p. 43.

The tassels are made of the same silk, by the method shown on p. 42.

69

Housewife cover

A cover of linen, embroidered in self colour with geometrical patterns in Satin, Eyelet, Fishbone, Double running and Double back stitches. The edges are joined with Bullion stitch and the cover fastened with buttons and loops. The filling is cedar dust. $3\frac{1}{4} \times 3\frac{1}{4}$ inches (8.5×8.5 cm).

Materials
Evenweave linen: Approximately 9×6 inches (23×15 cm) for the outer cover; linen or sateen for the inner cover, about $3\frac{1}{2} \times 7$ inches (9×18 cm).
Thread: Sewing cotton or linen. Linen thread for embroidery, buttons and loops. Filling, cedar dust or any filling available.

To make the inner cover
Two pieces should be sewn together on the wrong side to measure $3\frac{1}{4} \times 3\frac{1}{4}$ (8.5×8.5 cm) finished with an opening on one side. Turned right side out, the pad is filled and joined neatly.

To make the outer cover (Fig. 130)
This is made in one piece, the patterns marked and the folds defined, to make the housewife shape; the front only is embroidered, one quarter of which is given (Fig. 131).

With the embroidery completed, the turnings are made, and hemmed neatly on the wrong side. Turning to the right side, the hem is worked over with Double back stitch, as a border pattern.

129 Housewife cover

The cover is then folded in three, and the edges joined with short Bullion stitches. Three hand-made buttons (p. 40) are sewn just inside the under fold, and three button loops made on the edge of the front section, spaced to fit the buttons.

130 The outer cover

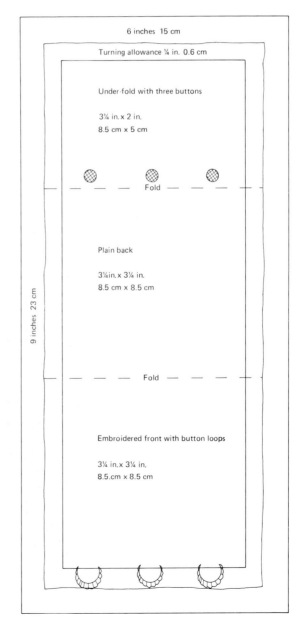

6 inches 15 cm

Turning allowance ¼ in. 0.6 cm

Under-fold with three buttons

3¼ in. x 2 in.
8.5 cm x 5 cm

Fold

Plain back

3¼ in. x 3¼ in.
8.5 cm x 8.5 cm

9 inches 23 cm

Fold

Embroidered front with button loops

3¼ in. x 3¼ in.
8.5 cm x 8.5 cm

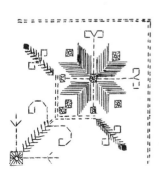

131

Envelope cover

A square linen outer cover, of an envelope type, with patterns worked throughout in Double running with black silk. The flap is fastened with a button and loop and the cover finished with a tassel of natural coloured and black silk thread. Filling, wool. 3 × 3 inches (8 × 8 cm).

Materials
Evenweave linen: About 12 × 6 inches (30 × 15 cm) for the outer cover, and the same amount for the lining of it; sateen or fine calico could be used instead. These can be used for the inner cover also, but the original is of fine linen; 8 × 4 inches will be needed (20 × 10 cm).
Threads: Black silk. White or natural sewing linen or cotton. Button-hole twist. A small ring for the button. Filling, wool.

To make the inner cover
Two pieces of material 4 × 4 inches (10 × 10 cm), should be joined on the wrong side, leaving an opening for filling. Turning it right side out, the cover should be filled to make a firm pad and the opening joined neatly.

132 Envelope cover

To make the outer cover (Fig. 133)
This can be made in three pieces and joined but is more economical of material, if marked and worked in one piece. The plan should be made by counting the threads; the original is worked over two threads of fine single-thread linen.

The middle section has a more elaborate pattern than the ends. One quarter of the plan for it is shown in Fig. 134.

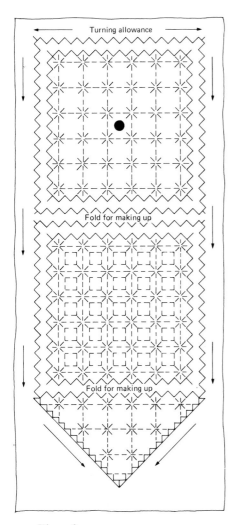

133 Plan of outer cover

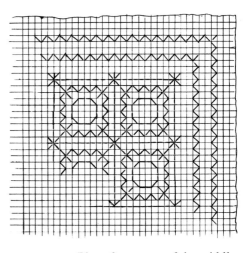

134 Plan of a quarter of the middle section

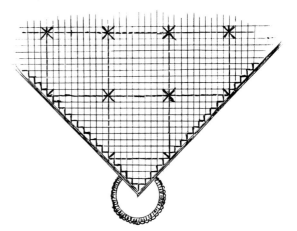

135 The pattern on the end sections with the position of the button loop .

To make up the cover (Fig. 136)

With the embroidery completed, the lining should be shaped and tacked to the wrong side of the cover, and the turnings of the embroidered section folded over its edges and hemmed down. The corner pieces marked A, may be left on and folded to make a firmer flap for fastening.

The lined cover is then folded in three like an envelope and the edges joined by close oversewing with black silk.

The cover is fastened with a button loop and a small wheel button (p. 40), sewn to the middle of the opposite end, after checking the position with the pad inside.

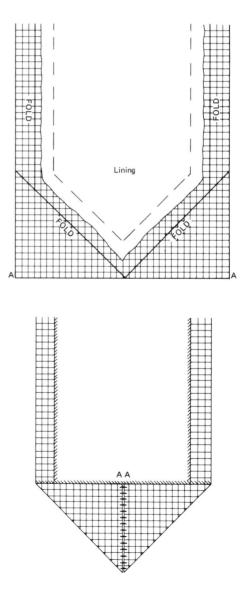

136

Circular cover

A circular box type of cover of linen worked in red silk and linen thread with Double running, Satin and Bullion stitches. The fastening is a red silk cord threaded through buttonhole loops finished with a bar button. Filling, wool. Diameter 3 inches (8 cm), depth 1 inch (2.5 cm).

Materials
Evenweave linen: About 11 × 7 inches (29 × 18 cm). The same amount of linen, sateen or calico for an under cover.
Thread: Coloured embroidery silk or stranded cotton. Sewing and tacking cottons.
Filling: wool.

To make the inner cover
Two circular pieces, $3\frac{1}{2}$ inches (9 cm) in diameter and a strip $10\frac{1}{2} \times 1\frac{1}{2}$ inches (25.5 × 4 cm) should be cut, and turnings made and tacked on

137 Circular cover

the wrong side. The edges should be nicked at intervals to ease the turning. (Figs. 138 and 139.)

The strip should then be sewn to the circular pieces by oversewing on the wrong side, leaving an opening for filling (Fig. 140).

The cover should be turned right side out and filled, sewing the opening neatly.

To make the top cover
One circle and the strip are embroidered.

With the embroidery completed (Satin stitch only on the edge of the base), the pieces should be cut out and turnings tacked on the wrong side. Buttonhole loops are then added round the edge of the base, and along one edge of the strip.

138 Cutting guide

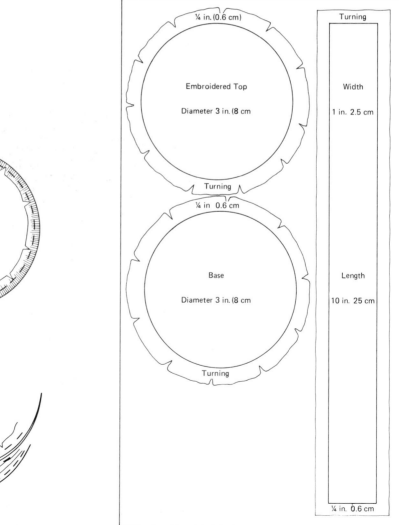

¼ in. (0.6 cm)

Embroidered Top

Diameter 3 in. (8 cm

Turning

¼ in 0.6 cm

Base

Diameter 3 in. (8 cm

Turning

Turning

Width

1 in. 2.5 cm

Length

10 in. 25 cm

¼ in. 0.6 cm

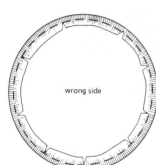

139

wrong side

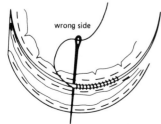

wrong side

140

To make up the cover

The top and side strip are joined by making short Bullion stitches at intervals, sewn through the Satin stitched edges (Fig. 143).

The pad should be fitted into the top part of the cover and the looped edges on the strip and base joined by threading them with a fine twisted cord, made from the embroidery silk or a matching thread (p. 43), which is finished with two small bar buttons. The cores of the buttons are made from linen thread, and bound with red silk (p. 41).

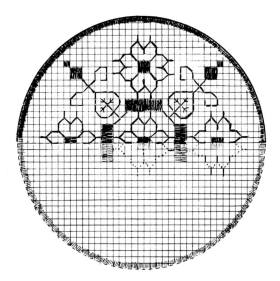

141 Half of the pattern for the top

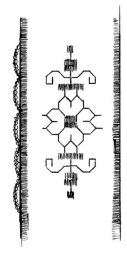

142 One of four identical patterns on the strip

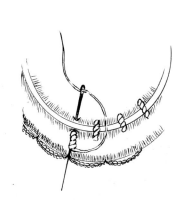

143 Joining the top and side with short Bullion stitches

Souvenirs, gifts and love tokens

For several hundred years, pincushions have been made as tokens of affection, esteem and remembrance, to mark a number of occasions. An appropriate inscription, the initials of the maker or receiver, and the date, often are among the decorations, popular kinds having been shell-decorated, knitted and pin-stuck patterns.

Cockle-shell pincushion

The cockle-shell pincushion in Fig. 145 is covered with moss green corded silk and stuck between a pair of cockle shells. An attached label reads – 'Marg⟨ᵗ⟩ Lawson Ford from Aunt Elizabeth Yealand. May 1877'. The filling is probably cotton wool.

Cockle and limpet shells were used in pairs with a small cushion stuck between them. The cushion consists of a round bag of stuffing, tied at the neck, with the ends trimmed as short as possible; it is stuck with adhesive into the shells, so as to hide the cut edges (Fig. 144). The shell edges are painted with gilt paint or covered with gold-coloured paper.

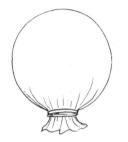

144 A round bag of stuffing forms the cushion

145 *left* Cockleshell pincushion *right* Shell-decorated box pincushion

Shell decorated box pincushion

The shell decorated box pincushion in Fig. 145 is a commercial souvenir, bought in Weston-super-Mare in 1926 for 4d. The cushion is covered with dark green velveteen, stuck in a box-shape of card, decorated with sea-shells. (39) The base is covered with unidentifiable tartan paper. Filling, probably sawdust or cotton wool. Height $2\frac{1}{2}$ inches (6.5 cm). Base 2×2 inches (5×5 cm).

Materials
A small cardboard box. Extra card, cut to shape; this is only necessary if an elaborate shape is fancied, but a plain box can be decorated just as well. Thick card for the base is needed.
Coloured paper. Clear adhesive, such as Bostik. Gold or silver paint. Polymer paint instead of paper, can be used for colouring the box shape. Velvet for the cushion; sawdust or wool for stuffing.

To make
The base should be cut slightly larger than the box, $\frac{1}{4}$ to $\frac{1}{2}$ inch (0.5 to 1.5 cm) is enough. Both should be covered with coloured paper stuck on, or painted with Polymer paint. The box should then be stuck to the base.

While the adhesive is drying, a well-stuffed velvet cushion should be made to fit the inside of the box, finishing level with the top and secured with a little adhesive to the bottom of the box.

When the adhesive is dry and hard the shells can be stuck to the outside of the box and base, beginning with an evenly matched row to mask the join. Each shell should be well coated on the back with adhesive and pressed gently into position.

Nail varnish remover can be used to remove accidents, or surplus on the fingers; the point of a penknife also can be used to remove Bostik while it is still elastic, but care should be taken not to remove a shell too.

A light coat of clear varnish should be applied to the shells to finish. This helps to keep them clean, as they are unequalled as dust-catchers.

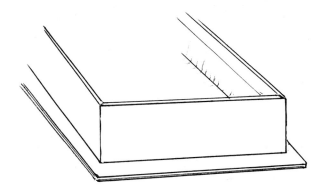

146 The base should be $\frac{1}{4}$ inch to $\frac{1}{2}$ inch larger than the box

Knitted pincushion covers

The patterns for pincushions knitted with Stocking stitch, as opposed to those in knitted lace (p. 18), were taken from Cross stitch designs, on especially made samplers intended for them, and not from knitting instruction books.

Letters and numerals also were taken from Cross stitch alphabets. No. 20 steel knitting needles were used, using 2 balls of silk of different colours.

To make a cover

Covers are knitted in two halves and the number of stitches varies according to the chosen pattern and colours. The usual number to cast on for each half is 14 stitches. Using two needles, knit 14, and turn. Make 1, purl 14. Turn, make 1, knit 15. Repeat, increasing 1 at the beginning of each row, until 60 stitches are on the needle. Knit and purl alternate rows without increase for 10 rows. The next row is decreased by 1 at the beginning, and each succeeding row is similarly decreased until 14 stitches are left, and cast off.

The chosen pattern is repeated or varied for the other side, which must be identical in size.

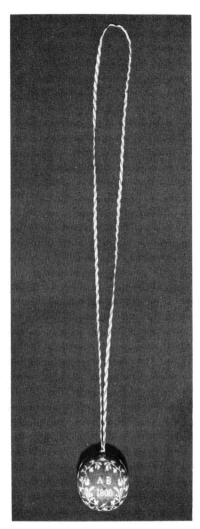

147 A pin-ball. The cover is knitted in cream and brown silks, mounted over a ball of padding, probably cotton wool. The hanging cord was plaited with matching silks (p. 44). The cushion is double-sided. 'A.B. 1800' and a wreath decorate the front. Diameter 1½ inches, circumference 6 inches (4 × 15 cm)

148 A typical knitting pattern for a pincushion taken from a sampler made by Eliza Trusted in 1803 and copied many times since then

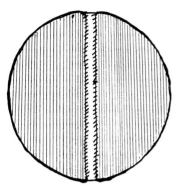

149 Pad of the pinball with covers

To make up a pin ball

A pad is made by rolling cotton wool between the hands, into a firm ball and large enough for the covers to be stretched over it for a close fit. Each half should meet in the middle of the pad, and be sewn on separately.

The join is covered with ribbon or plaited silk, which can be extended to make a loop for hanging (p. 44).

150 Eighteenth-century pinballs with needlewoven covers, worked in silk thread with different patterns

Flat circular knitted pincushion

A double-sided cushion, knitted with cream and dark green silks, by a pupil at Ackworth School in Yorkshire, about the middle of the nineteenth century. The inscription 'FROM ACKWORTH SCHOOL' is on the front, with a reverse pattern of four formal trees. (Fig. 153.) The top and base are mounted on cards over a flannel pad, bound at the edges with ribbon. Diameter 2 inches, depth $\frac{1}{2}$ inch (5×1.5 cm).

To make the cushion
The knitting is the same as for a pinball, using silk of two colours and fine needles.

When both sides are completed, each is stretched over a circle of card, 2 inches in diameter (5 cm), and the turnings at the back stitched with Back stitches (Fig. 152).

To make up the cushion
A pad is made by rolling a half-inch wide strip of flannel (1.5 cm), until a pad 2 inches wide (5 cm) is made. This should be stitched to prevent unrolling.

The sides should be covered with tape or binding and kept in place by Back stitching each fold (Fig. 154).

The stiffened covers for the top and base should then be attached to the pad, by sewing the edges to the bind (Fig. 155).

The cushion should be finished by covering the edges with silk ribbon, tied in a flat bow (Fig. 156).

151 Flat circular knitted pincushion

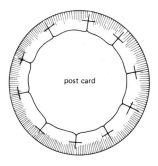

152 The top and base are stiffened with card

153 The reverse pattern on the pincushion from Ackworth School

154

155

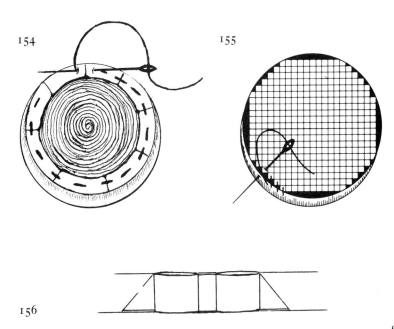

156

Pin-stuck maternity or christening pincushions

A maternity pincushion was a social necessity, regardless of class, in an eighteenth- or nineteenth-century layette. Made before the baby's arrival by, or as a gift for the mother, the pin-stuck inscriptions were non-committal, referring to the infant as 'little stranger' or 'sweet babe' and so on, and giving no more than the year of the expected arrival, to cover eventualities.

Maternity cushion

The cover is of fine cream piqué, with a double frill of cambric. The initials of the father (top line), and mother, WELCOME SWEET BABE, 1826, are surrounded by a running spray of leaves, which are marked with still untarnished pins. (The babe lived to be 86.) Filling, wool. $6\frac{1}{4} \times 5\frac{1}{2}$ inches (15.5×14 cm).

Materials
About 14×7 inches white or cream material (not velvet). At least 1 yard of fine material, ribbon, or lace, 2 inches wide (5 cm) for the frill. Thin tracing or tissue paper. Brass pins, not steel.

157 Alphabets and numerals taken from Cross-stitch patterns used for maternity cushions, inscriptions and dates. Capitals

158 Minuscule alphabet and numerals

To make the cover

The material should be cut into two pieces, turnings made and tacked on the wrong side, to give a finished size of $6\frac{1}{4} \times 5\frac{1}{2}$ inches (15.5×14 cm). They should be joined by oversewing, leaving an opening for filling. Turning the cover right side out, the cushion should be firmly stuffed, making sure the corners are filled, and the opening neatly joined.

To make the frill

If material is used, a piece of at least a yard (90 cm) in length, 2 inches (5 cm) wide should be cut and hemmed with the narrowest possible

159 Maternity cushion

turning, to make a width of $1\frac{3}{4}$ inches (4.5 cm). Wide ribbon needs no hem and double the amount of lace would be needed, 2 yards.

Two parallel rows of even Running stitches should be made, the stitches in each being equal and opposite to one another, and the rows being one inch from one edge and $\frac{3}{4}$ inch from the other (Fig. 160).

The gathers should be drawn up until the frill fits the cushion. Folding along the gathered line, the frill is hemmed along the fold to the edges of the cushion, with the narrower frill in front.

To mark the patterns
The whole pattern with any initials, dates or inscriptions should be drawn or traced with pencil on the paper cut to the size of the cushion top.

To pin-stick the patterns
Following the pencilled lines, the pins should be put in at right angles to the surface, so that the heads lie flat. Spacing must be even, without the pin-heads touching; they must never overlap.

If the pin is slanted, the head is tipped and the pattern spoiled.

When the pattern is completed, the paper should be torn away with care and without disturbance to the pins, although adjustments can be made afterwards.

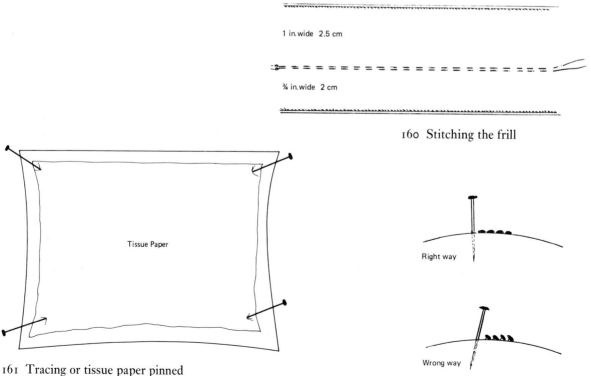

1 in. wide 2.5 cm

¾ in. wide 2 cm

160 Stitching the frill

Tissue Paper

161 Tracing or tissue paper pinned in position

Right way

Wrong way

162 Sticking in the pins

163 A seventeenth-century
pin-stuck satin pincushion. This is
an early example of a pincushion
with pin-stuck patterns which are
typical of the embroidery done at
that time. It is not known whether
the initials 'AE' are those of the
maker, or the person for whom the
work was done, but there is no
disputing the date

164 A tracing taken from a
maternity cushion made about 1850

Another maternity cushion

This small oval satin pincushion (6 × 5 inches, 15 × 13 cm) is one in which the patterns and inscriptions differ from the usual. The inscription is in copperplate letters, with pin-heads touching the cushion top. The pins in the garland are of two sizes, those with larger than usual heads in the stem patterns and small fine pins for the leaves. Also, instead of the pin-heads resting on the material, they are raised about one eighth of an inch (3 mm) above it, so that the inscription is on a lower level.

The method of pin-sticking is the same as for the previous cushion. The edges are finished with a bought silk fringe.

165 Maternity cushion

Beaded pin-stuck cushions

Beaded pin-stuck cushions were considered suitable gifts from absent friends in the nineteenth century, especially those serving in the Army and Navy, and also from tongue-tied young men and girls nearer home, who were able so to declare their feelings openly without saying a word. Heart-shaped cushions and patterns of hearts were a matter of course, whatever other decoration was worked out in pins and beads as well as ribbon, braid, sequins, lace and fringes.

Pin-stuck heart cushions

A pair of heart-shaped blue velveteen cushions, decorated with pink satin panels, and inscriptions pinned in white beads 'TRUE LOVE' and 'THINK OF ME'. Anchor patterns suggest they were made by a sailor. Other decorations are borders of metal thread and blue beads, white cotton fringe and paper scraps of pansies. Filling, probably sawdust. Width 5 inches, length 4 inches (12.5 × 10 cm).

Materials for each cushion
Pieces of cotton velveteen at least 7 × 6 inches (18 × 15 cm) to allow for turnings. Scraps of satin, metal thread or lurex. Beads with holes large enough to take pins. Fringe. Sewing cotton. Brass pins, not steel which will rust. Sawdust or wool.

166 Pin-stuck heart cushions

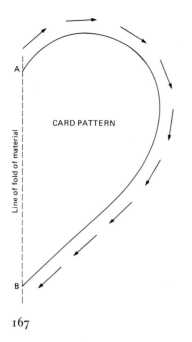

A

Line of fold of material

CARD PATTERN

B

167

To make the cushion

The size and outline should be decided, and a half-heart cut out in cardboard accordingly (Fig. 167).

The velvet should be folded on the straight, *wrong side out*, and the half-heart laid on the fold.

With a white or light coloured pencil, the outline of the heart should be drawn on to the velvet, and allowing at least an inch (2.5 cm) outside the outline for turning, the shape should be cut out from A to B. When unfolded, the heart pattern will be complete. Repeat for the other side.

With the two pieces held together wrong side out, they should be tacked, then machined or backstitched exactly along the white pencil lines, leaving an opening for filling. The outside edge of the turning allowances should be slightly nicked, and then the cover turned right side out. When the filling is firmly packed in, the opening should be neatly joined.

168 Cut 2 heart-shaped pieces with a 1 inch (2.5 cm) turning allowance

Pinsticking

Inscriptions, names and dates nearly always are done with block letters and numerals on beaded pin-stuck cushions.

To pin-stick the patterns

The proposed arrangement of the patterns should be traced or drawn on to thin tracing or tissue paper, cut in the shape of the heart, and pinned to the cushion top.

Each pin is put through a bead first, and then stuck in its appropriate place in the pattern (Fig. 170).

The border pattern on both cushions, is made by taking the metal thread behind each pin, before it is pushed in (Fig. 171).

The fringe is sewn on.

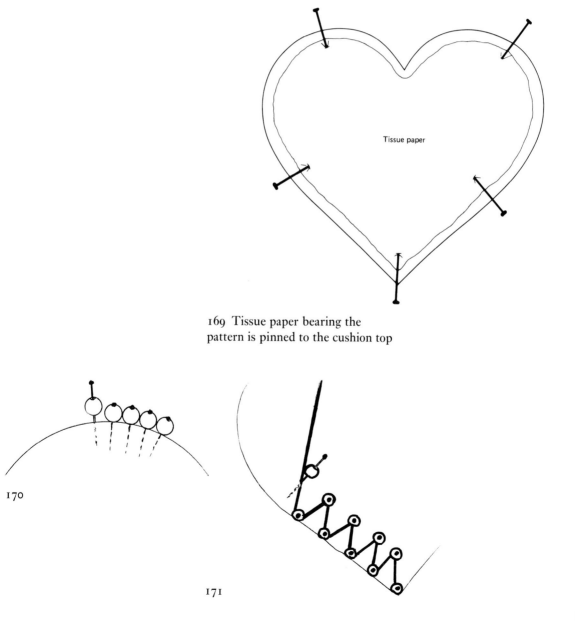

Tissue paper

169 Tissue paper bearing the pattern is pinned to the cushion top

170

171

Beaded pin-stuck cushion

A gift made by a soldier during the Boer War for his son. The cover is of dark green velvet and the inscription and patterns are pin-stuck with multi-coloured beads. The pin-heads are very large. The crossed swords and rifles, the cross crown anchor and (supposedly) regimental crest, are typical of patterns on pincushions made by servicemen. A repaired slit in the back cover, was made when savings kept in the cushion, were removed. Filling, coarse sawdust. 6 × 4 inches (15 × 10 cm).

To make the cushion
Except for the shape, the planning of the pattern and carrying out the pin-sticking, is the same as that for the heart-shaped cushions.

It is usual for a fringe or cord to have been added as a finish and some soldier's and sailor's cushions are so elaborately made that the original cover of the cushion cannot be seen.

172 Beaded pin-stuck cushion

Bead-embroidered pincushions

The difference between a useful and a useless beaded top-cover lies in the space allowed for the purpose of keeping pins in it. Sometimes, the work clearly has taken charge of the worker, but when purpose and decoration share the available space, nothing can look better. Bead-decorated covers, other than embroidered and pin-stuck ones, have been made also with knitting, loom-weaving and needle weaving with beads, as well as beaded net and lace.

Beaded velvet pincushion

The round purple velvet cover is embroidered with a running garland of flower, leaf and bud patterns, using clear glass and pearl beads, fish scales and gold-coloured silk twist. A twisted loop fringe of glass beads and a silk cord are sewn to the edges. 6 inches in diameter (15 cm), $1\frac{1}{2}$ inches (4 cm) deep.

Materials
Velvet: About 8×8 inches (20×20 cm). Satin or sateen for the under cover. Iron-on vilene.
Thread: Gold or purple coloured sewing silk. Gold-coloured silk twist. Sewing cotton. Wool for filling. Small embroidery frame.
Beads, medium and small sizes. Sequins instead of fish-scales.

173 Beaded velvet pincushion

To make the under cover

Two circles of satin or sateen should be cut out, 7 inches (18 cm) in diameter, and a strip, 20 × 2½ inches (50 × 6 cm).

Also, one circle of thick iron-on vilene, 6 inches diameter (15 cm) and a strip 19 × 1½ inches (48 × 4 cm).

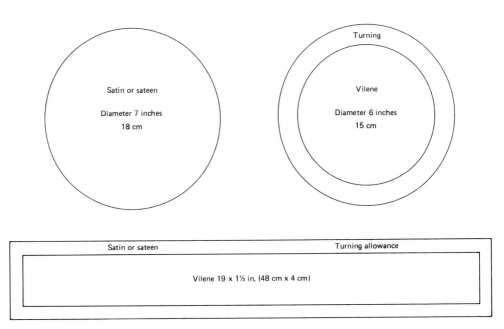

Satin or sateen

Diameter 7 inches
18 cm

Turning

Vilene

Diameter 6 inches
15 cm

Satin or sateen   Turning allowance

Vilene 19 x 1½ in. (48 cm x 4 cm)

174 Pattern pieces

The vilene pieces should be ironed on to the wrong side of the strip and one circle of satin, allowing for turnings. Turnings should be tacked on these and the other circle on the wrong side.

The strip should be joined to both circles by oversewing on the right side, leaving an opening for filling. The cover should then be stuffed, keeping the sides as flat as possible, and the opening joined.

To make the top cover

Bead embroidery should be worked in an embroidery frame, but if one is not available, a small piece of work can be pinned to the back of a light picture frame (Fig. 175). A double ring frame is not suitable for velvet as it marks the pile.

The outline of the top and the design for beading can be marked on the velvet with tacking or running stitches in white thread, and the stem sewn on first, with couching (Fig. 176).

The flower and other patterns can then be sewn in their appropriate positions. Sequins can be used instead of fish-scales, and are sewn on through the holes drilled in them (Fig. 177).

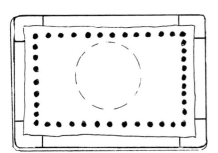

175 The top cover pinned to a frame

The pearls are sewn on singly or in clusters of six or four (each sewn separately) for the flower centres. The 'buds' consist of one small bead and a larger one sewn on together (Fig. 178).

When the beading is completed and the velvet removed from the frame, the circle should be cut out, with a good turning allowance, and hemmed to the top edge of the cushion.

To make the fringe

This fringe can be made by stringing two threads of clear glass beads, and attaching them to the top edge alternately (Fig. 179), twisting the loops before stitching.

A hand-made cord (p. 43) is added as a finish.

176 Sewing on the stem pattern

177 Sequins form the flower pattern

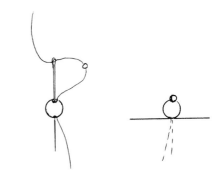

178 Sewing on the pearls

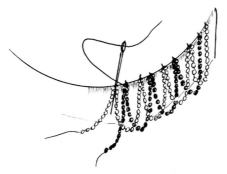

179 Sewing on the beaded fringe

Beaded fan pincushion

The decoration is made almost entirely of pale green and gold-coloured sequins in a variety of shapes, with some small amethyst coloured glass beads and green buttonhole twist, on a cream watered-silk ground. The reverse side is undecorated and the top of the pad contains twelve pearl-headed pins. Filling, layers of wool fabric. Curved top $5\frac{1}{4}$ inches (13.5 cm), sides $2\frac{3}{4}$ inches (7 cm).

Materials
Silk: About 8×8 inches (20×20 cm). Scraps of flannel or wool fabric for the pad. Card for stiffening.
Selection of sequins and small beads. Pale green buttonhole twist. Cream sewing silk. Sewing cotton.

To bead the cover
The pattern should be lightly marked on the silk with running stitches in sewing silk, which should then be put into a small frame for beading (Fig. 181).

The pattern is begun by couching the 'stems' with the buttonhole twist.

Circular sequins are drilled with a centre hole, and those used for the radiating lines are sewn through the holes and over the edges at each side.

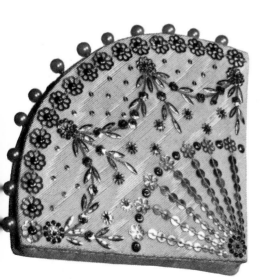

180 Beaded fan pincushion

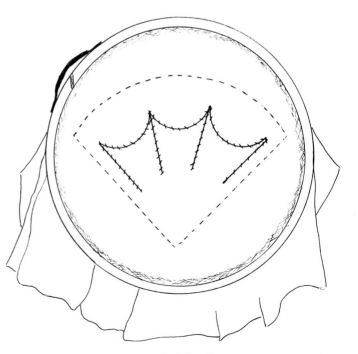

181 The silk in a frame for beading

96

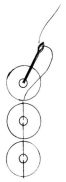

182 Attaching lines of sequins

Single circular sequins are attached by sewing a bead in the centre.

The oval leaf shapes, which are drilled at each end, are sewn on with 2 beads.

To make up the cushion

The beaded top should be removed from the frame and any marking stitches which can be seen should be taken out. The piece, with another of similar shape for the back of the cushion, should be cut out and the turning allowances nicked on the rounded edges.

They should both be sewn to cards cut to shape.

The pad should be made by sewing together layers of flannel to the thickness of $\frac{1}{4}$ inch (0.5 cm), trimmed to the shape and size of the covered cards, and the edges bound with pieces of watered silk or cream ribbon.

The front and back of the cushions are hemmed neatly with cream sewing silk, to the binding of the pad.

The pincushion is finished with 12 pearl-headed beads in the curved top.

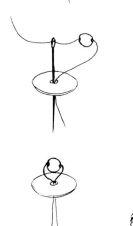

183 Attaching single sequins

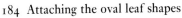

184 Attaching the oval leaf shapes

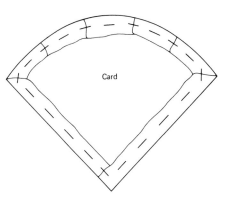

185 The top and base are stiffened with card

186 Layers of flannel form the pad

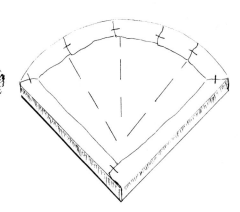

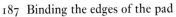

187 Binding the edges of the pad

97

Beaded patchwork pincushions

These two pincushions made in the 1880s are a type of many pocket pincushions in use at the time. Each hexagonal piece is of silk, no two of the same colour. The beads are sewn on in one-colour strings of five or six beads, each string ending in a white bead, which makes a uniform pattern. The pins were kept at the edges. Filling, sheep's wool. Width 2 inches (5 cm).

To make a cushion
This type is always double sided, needing fourteen hexagonal ½ inch pieces (1.5 cm), to complete a cushion.

Each piece is made by the usual method for patchwork (p. 101) but the papers are left in. The beading is done after the cushion is stuffed and made up, and each hexagon is beaded separately.

To begin, a threaded needle, with a small knot in the thread, is inserted into the cushion, in an angle between two hexagons, at the edge, coming out at the exact centre of the middle hexagon (Fig. 189).

Five beads should then be threaded, and working from right to left, a stitch made from one corner of the hexagon to the next, drawing the beads into position with the thread (Fig. 190).

Threading five more beads, the needle is inserted again in the middle hexagon, coming out at the next corner (Fig. 191).

This is continued until six strings have been sewn and the same pattern repeated on the other side.

To finish, pins are put in round the edges.

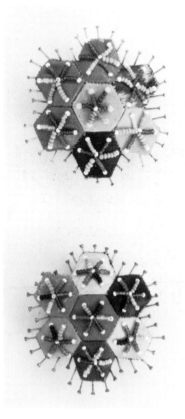

188 Beaded patchwork pincushions

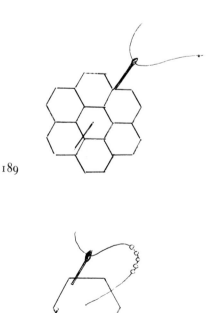

189

190   191

192 A nineteenth-century teapot pincushion. Made of sky-blue satin, it has panels of royal blue satin embroidered with flower patterns in coloured beads framed in 'gold'. The brim of the lid, which is removable, is encrusted with a garland of bead flowers, also bordered with gold beads, and the cushion itself is crowned with an elaborate bead butterfly with antennae of horsehair. The hollow interior is lined with yellow sateen and is roomy enough to hold thimble, needles and tape measure. It stands as firm as a rock, and if it would hold tea, it could be poured through the hollow spout. Height about 4 inches

193 Nineteenth-century beaded pinstuck pincushion. The background material is blue velvet decorated with red and white ribbon and gold thread, held in place with pinstuck beads and imitation pearls. The base is 10 × 10 inches (25 × 25 cm) and the height at the centre is 8 inches (20 cm)

99

Patchwork pincushions

Pincushion covers made of patchwork are very hard-wearing, especially if they are made of cotton, sateen, dress cottons or chintz, whether printed or plain, and if stuffed with wool. Silk (especially tie-silk), satin, and velvet also are suitable, but not so easy to handle. The methods used are those associated with quilt making, and the geometrical patterns, although smaller in scale, also are similar and include pieces of three-, four-, five-, six-, and eight-sided shapes.

Three hexagonal patchwork pincushions

Materials
Scraps of coloured cottons or viyella. Paper or thin iron-on vilene. Coloured stranded and sewing cottons. Sheep's wool. Templates (p. 120). Pairs of matching small hexagonal and lozenge shapes.

To prepare the pieces
These pincushions are stronger with patchwork on both sides, and calculations should be made for this when cutting the pieces. Both shapes are made by the same method. The width of each hexagonal piece is half an inch (1.5 cm).

Using the solid template of each shape as a guide, the paper or vilene should be cut from them. Cutting should be done at the edges of the template and not from pencil lines drawn round.

Using the frame templates, an equal number of fabric pieces should be cut out. Pencil lines drawn round the outside edge of this template can be used.

194 Three hexagonal patchwork pincushions
top left Hexagon and lozenge shapes cut from colour-printed cotton of light and mid-blue, and black and white, finished at the edges with blue threads couched with black. 4 inches across (10 cm)
right Hexagonal and lozenge shapes cut from green, grey and black and white printed dress cottons, finished at the edges with green threads couched with black. $3\frac{1}{2}$ inches across (9 cm)
centre Hexagonal pieces only, cut from blue, brown and white printed viyella. Finished at the edges with white threads couched with brown. $2\frac{1}{2}$ inches across (6.5 cm)

Each patch is made by covering a paper or vilene shape with a matching piece of material. The paper can be pinned, and the vilene should be ironed, to the wrong side, and each covered by turning the material over the edges and tacking the folds.

The pieces are joined on the wrong side. The seams should be well made, or they will gape when the stuffing is done.

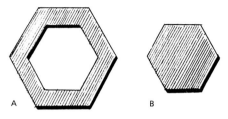

195 Pair of lozenge-shaped templates

196 Pair of hexagonal templates

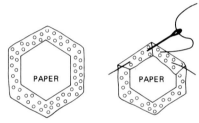

197 Stages of making a hexagon

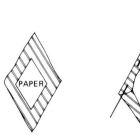

198 Stages of making a lozenge

199 Joining hexagons

200 Joining lozenges

201 Joining a hexagon and a lozenge

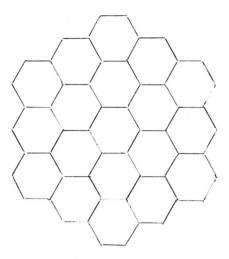

Before joining all the patches, it is well to arrange them in a plan to check the pattern.

The patterns on both sides need not be identical, as long as the number of pieces is the same for each, so that the edges match up for joining.

To make the cushion

When the top and base covers are completed, the tacking and papers should be removed from all the patches. Vilene is left in. Then holding both covers together, with the right sides outwards, the edges are joined by oversewing, but leaving an opening on one corner, for stuffing (Fig. 205). The turnings of the unjoined section should be tacked to keep them in shape while stuffing.

A stuffing stick will be needed for stuffing and the sheep's wool cut, to fill the corners. The opening should be joined neatly.

202 A plan for the small cushion. 19 hexagonal pieces for each side, 38 pieces in all

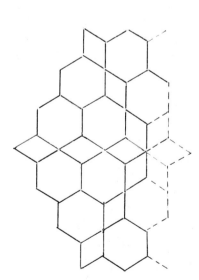

203 The planned layout of pieces for half of one side for the cushion at top left in Fig. 194. 18 hexagonal pieces and 18 lozenges for each side, making a total of 36 of each shape

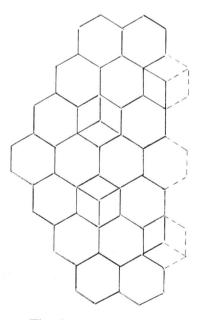

204 The planned layout of pieces for half of one side for the cushion on the right in Fig. 194. 31 hexagons and 18 lozenges are needed for each side, making a total of 62 hexagons and 36 lozenges

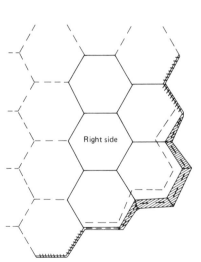

Right side

205

The edges of the cushion can be finished by couching 3 or 4 strands of stranded cotton over the joining stitches (Fig. 206). This gives the appearance of a fine cord round the edges of the cushion.

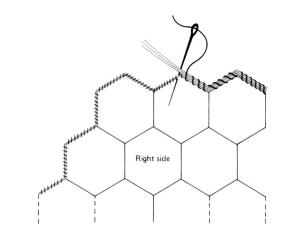

206

Square patchwork pincushion

Although this cushion is as shallow as a mattress cushion, it is not sewn through. The patchwork is made of half-inch squares (1.5 × 1.5 cm) of scarlet and white striped, spotted and plain dress cottons. The sides are stiffened, and joined to the top and base by fine piping cord, covered with scarlet chintz. Filling, pieces of unworn blanket. $4 \times 4 \times \frac{1}{2}$ inches (10 × 10 × 1.5 cm).

207 Square patchwork cushion

208 A pair of square templates

Materials
Scraps of dress cottons and light furnishing cottons.
Fine piping cord. Iron-on vilene, thick and thin. Paper. Pieces of unworn blanket or tweed. Sewing cotton.
A pair of square templates.

To prepare the pieces
The pattern is made of 64 half-inch squares; 32 one-inch squares could also be used to make a different pattern for a cushion of the same size.

Using the solid template as a guide, paper or vilene squares should be cut – 64 pieces for each side, 128 in all.

Using the hollow template, an equal number of fabric pieces should be cut, from pencil lines drawn round the outer edge. Square pieces also can be cut by folding the material into squares and cutting along the folds.

Each piece is made by covering a paper or vilene shape with a square of material. The paper can be pinned, or the vilene ironed to the wrong side of the material, and covered by turning the material over the edges and tacking the folds.

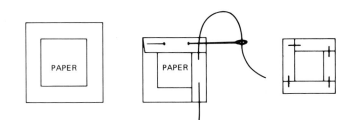

209 The stages of making a square piece

Before joining the pieces, it is as well to arrange them in a plan to check the pattern. Also, a pad should be made, half an inch (1.5 cm) thick, of layers of blanket or table felt stitched together and trimmed to size, 4 × 4 inches (10 × 10 cm).

Four pieces of thick vilene, each 4 inches long and half an inch wide (10 × 1.5 cm) should be ironed on to four strips of material for the sides, which have been cut with turning allowances.

The turnings are made and sewn down lightly on the wrong side, and the strips are joined together at the ends.

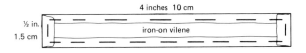

210 The side pieces (Cut 4)

The strips are then finished by sewing covered piping cord to the edges, and hemming them to the top and base covers, as for the mattress pincushion on p. 53, leaving one edge open for putting in the pad. The opening should be neatly hemmed up.

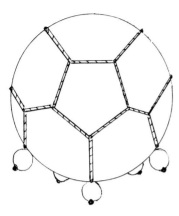

211 Patchwork pin-ball

Patchwork pin-ball

The sketch in Fig. 211 is of a present day copy of the same kind of nineteenth-century patchwork pin-balls which were made to be kept in the workbox (p. 109). The construction is the same and it is made of pentagonal pieces of felt in shades of green and brown, with gilt lurex cord (off a chocolate box) couched over the seams. Five large beads are attached to the base with glass-headed pins, to act as feet to prevent the cushion rolling. Circumference 8 inches (20 cm). Filling, wool ravellings.

Materials
Scraps of coloured felt. Sewing cotton, not white.
Wool ravellings or sheep's wool. 5 large beads. 5 large pins.
Pentagonal template.

To make the template
This five-sided shape is so easy to make that any size can be cut as needed, without the expense of buying one.

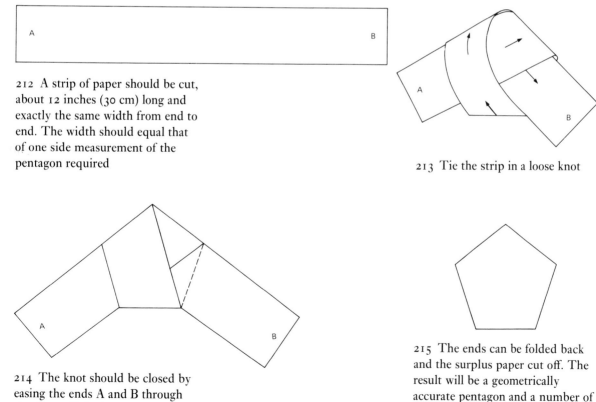

212 A strip of paper should be cut, about 12 inches (30 cm) long and exactly the same width from end to end. The width should equal that of one side measurement of the pentagon required

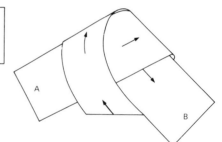

213 Tie the strip in a loose knot

214 The knot should be closed by easing the ends A and B through the tie, until the knot can be flattened into a 5-sided shape

215 The ends can be folded back and the surplus paper cut off. The result will be a geometrically accurate pentagon and a number of working templates of card should be cut from the outline

To make and join the pieces

To make and join the pieces

If a material other than felt is used, such as velvet, it is necessary to cut and cover paper or vilene pieces as usual for patchwork, but whatever the material, or the size of the pieces, only 12 are needed for the pincushion.

Twelve pieces of felt in assorted colours should be cut from the template, being careful not to shave the card at the edge with the scissors. It is not geometrically possible to make the pattern using only two colours, say black and white, without two pieces of similar colour coming together at one place.

The edges of each section can then be fitted together and joined, leaving an opening for stuffing. The work is not turned inside out, as the seams will be covered.

Stuffing must be done with care, as felt will stretch, but by holding the ball in the cupped palm of one hand, this will be avoided. The opening should be joined neatly and the cushion rolled between the hands a little to round it.

216 The pieces are joined by oversewing the cut edges of the felt pieces, as no turnings are needed. The first stage is made by joining two groups of six pieces which will lie flat

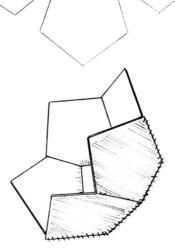

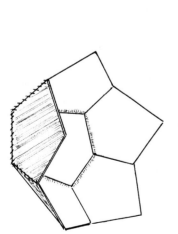

217a and b The sides of the surrounding pieces in each group are then joined, and should result in two cup-shaped sections

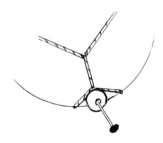

218 The seams are then covered with lurex or other fine cord, by couching, and 5 large beads attached by glass-headed pins to the 5 corners of one patch, on which the cushion will stand

Patchwork star pincushion

This pincushion is double-sided, made of five- and six-sided shapes in blue silk and velvet, and decorated with pink beads and tassels. Filling, wool. 4 inches (10 cm) from point to point.

To make the templates
The five-sided pieces can be cut from a card template, based on a hexagon, by outlining the hexagon to be used for the centre patches, with pencil on card.

The 2 sides of the hexagon top should be extended, until the lines meet in a point. This outline should be cut out, and iron-on vilene pieces cut from it.

219 Patchwork star pincushion

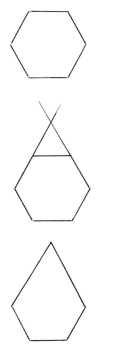

220 Making a five-sided template

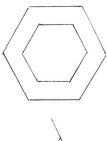

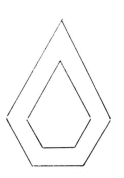

The same method should be used to make a template for cutting the fabric pieces.

Materials
Scraps of coloured silk and velvet. Assorted beads, including 6 large ones for tassels. Sewing silk, stranded cotton and wool for stuffing. Iron-on vilene.

To make the cushion
The usual procedure of covering vilene shapes, and tacking the turnings on the wrong side, is followed. One hexagonal piece of velvet and six five-sided shapes of silk are used for each side. These are joined by oversewing the seams on the wrong side to make a star shape (Fig. 222).

When both sides have been completed, they should be joined with oversewing along all sides, on the right side, leaving an opening for stuffing. A stuffing stick will be necessary to pack in the wool filling.

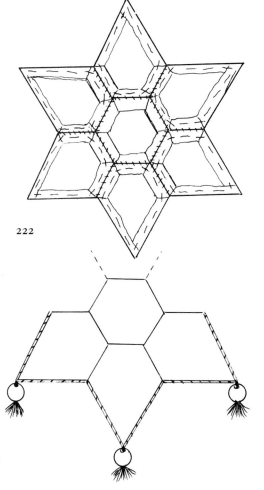

222

221 Five-sided template for the fabric pieces

223 The seams are covered with couched threads of coloured stranded cotton (p. 103) and a small tassel attached to each point (p. 42)

224 A cube shaped cushion made of black and white silk squares on each side. Decorated with pink and yellow beads, it resembles a liquorice allsort

225 A pin-ball made from eight long diamond-shaped pieces of blue and white silk decorated with blue and pearl beads. The pins are kept in the seams

A hassock or footstool pincushion

Of the many household articles represented as pincushions, the hassock at least was practical enough to be used and was considered suitably easy for a child to make. It is made of four triangular pieces of yellow and brown velvet joined to make the top, with black velvet ribbon round the sides and on the base. A gilt bead or small button in the centre is sewn through to the pad. (Plate opposite p. 72.)

To make the cushion – Figs 227, 228
The rounded sides are then turned in and sewn to 1 inch wide (2.5 cm) black velvet ribbon, on the right side, inserting two small folded pieces of velvet on each side as tabs, and sewing them in firmly.

A circle of card the same size as the top should be cut and covered with a circle of black velvet for the base.

A strip of flannel 1 inch wide (2.5 cm) should be rolled (30) until it is large enough to fit snugly into the circular top.

The velvet covered base should then be stitched to the lower edge of the ribbon, and all the edges covered with couched silk twist or fine lurex cord. A small button or decorative bead may be sewn on the top to cover the joining point of the pieces.

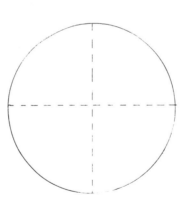

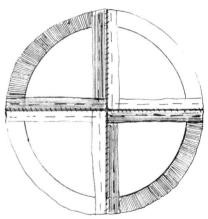

227 A circle of thick iron-on vilene should be quartered and cut out, and the pieces ironed on to the wrong side of the velvet. Any two colours can be used

228 The pieces should be cut with good turnings, and the straight sides of the triangles joined on the wrong side with oversewing

226 A pin-ball made of blue and dark red velvet pieces in the same method as the felt pin-ball (p. 105). The corners are decorated with gold-coloured pearl beads

Patchwork pincushions as decorations

So-called patchwork pincushions were made in great quantity in the nineteenth century, for sale at bazaars and sales of work. Although only a few were of use as pincushions, all contained pins even if they were just for decoration. Nowadays they are being copied as baubles for Christmas trees. They are made by the usual methods used in patchwork and will stand on their own feet, but a cord or ribbon is sometimes attached for hanging.

Star pincushion

Made of sixty lozenge shapes, covered with percale and joined in 12 sections. Each section is a different colour, red, dark greens, tan, olive green, russet, shrimp pink, cream and yellows. The points are pin-stuck with gilt beads, and the centres sewn with blue sequins. The edges are pin-stuck with yellow brass pins. 2 inches (5 cm) high.

Materials
Thin coloured cotton or silk. Card, beads, pins and templates (p. 120). A larger sized template will make a larger star; some are 6 inches high.

229 Star pincushion

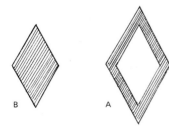

230 60 pieces of thin card should be cut from template B. Using template A as a guide, 60 pieces of material 5 each of 12 different colours should be cut out

To make the star

Like the pin-ball (p. 106) it is best to make the star in two halves (5 stars round a centre one) and join them afterwards.

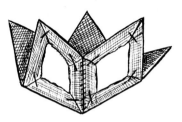

231 The cards should be covered, taking care not to allow tackings to show on the right side, and 5 lozenges of one colour should be joined to make each section

232 After they are joined to lie flat, the edges of the first and last lozenge are sewn together to make a cup-shaped star

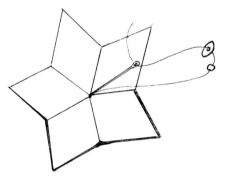

233 If a beaded sequin or other decoration is to be put in the centre, it should be done now

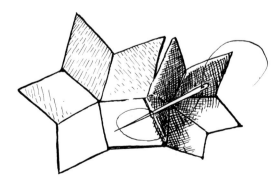

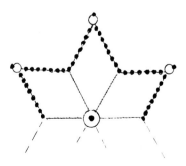

234 The sections should be joined by oversewing the edges on the right side

235 When complete, the edges and points are pinstuck

III

Another star pincushion

236 Star pincushion

Sixty triangular pieces are needed for the smaller star. Like the pieces in the other, they are covered with reddish pink, crimson and purple percale. All the joins and points are pin-stuck with pearl beads and yellow brass pins and the centres finished with a pin-stuck bead and sequin.

Materials
Thin, coloured cotton or silk. Card, pins, beads and templates (p. 120).
   Other pyramids are joined on to the bases of the five, and continued in this way, until the star is complete.

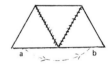

237 Templates for Star pincushion

238 The method used for making the triangles is the same as for the lozenges. The pieces are joined in groups of three

239 The broad ends of the first and third triangles are joined to make a hollow pyramid

240 Five pyramids are then joined at their bases, to make a star section

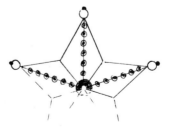

241 The seams and points are pinstuck with beads and the centres with pin-stuck sequins.

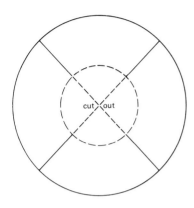

242 Cutting guide

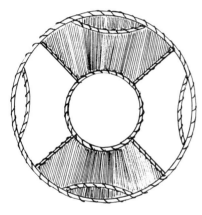

243a The pincushion completed
b One segment of the lifebelt
pincushion

A lifebelt pincushion

The lifebelt in a small size was suitable for hanging on the parlour wall, but larger ones were quite practical and were used on the dressing table, with a small vase of flowers in the centre.

Velvet or silk pieces of navy blue and white are joined to make a padded hollow circle, decorated with 'rope' made of white silk cord. Sometimes HMS PIN was pinstuck on the cushion.

To make the cushion
Two circles of iron-on vilene should be quartered, and before cutting out, a smaller circle marked in the centre of each. This is removed in the cutting out, to give the shaped segments.

The segments should be ironed on the wrong side of the material making four white and four blue pieces, allowing for turnings.

The turnings should be made and tacked on the wrong side but the tackings should not show on the right side. The circles are then joined together on the inner edges.

The outer edges are joined on the right side, leaving an opening for the stuffing of sheep's wool, or ravellings. When filled, the opening should be neatly joined and the 'rope' of silk cord sewn on over all the joins. Small loops of the cord can be added to the top also.

For use as a bauble, glitter can be added by decorating the inner and outer edges with pinstuck glass beads.

244 Lifebelt pincushion

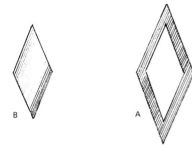

A daisy pincushion

The flower is made of a star of long diamond shapes used for patchwork, covered with thin white silk, surmounted by a round cushion of yellow velvet. The stem and leaves are covered with green silk. All the edges are sewn with small beads, and the other joins hidden with sequins.

To make the pincushion
These are joined in pairs on the right side. Two strips of card are similarly covered and joined for the stem, inserted in the flower and neatly joined. The leaves are joined to it at the other end.

A pad of yellow velvet stuffed with wool is sewn or can be stuck in the centre of the star. All the edges are beaded, with pink beads on the flower part and green ones on the leaves and pink sequins sewn round the pad. Lines of green silk can be couched on the leaves.

245 16 pieces of card cut from template B should be covered with 16 pieces of silk cut from template A

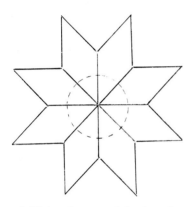

246 Eight pieces are joined on the wrong side to make a star shape, and the two stars are then joined together at the edges on the right side, leaving a small opening to insert the stem.

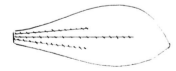

247 Four pieces of card are cut and covered with green silk for the leaves.

248 A daisy pincushion

A pansy pincushion

249 A pansy pincushion

The flower is made of purple velvet and yellow silk, the leaves and stem of light green velvet. Beading patterns are done with small glass beads and sequins and the edges of the flower are pin-stuck.

To make the pansy
Card should be cut to the shapes of the petals, for which bought templates are not available.

The appropriate pieces should be covered with purple velvet and yellow silk, and the leaves and stem with green velvet, and joined with oversewing on the wrong side, with matching sewing silk.

Both halves of the flower are joined on the edges on the right side, leaving an opening for the insertion of the stem, after which the opening should be firmly joined. The leaves should be joined at the other end of the stem.

The leaf edges are finished with couched threads of stranded cotton and any joins covered with beaded sequins.

250 4 pieces are needed for the top half

251 2 pieces for the bottom centre

252 8 pieces for the sides

253 4 pieces for the 2 leaves

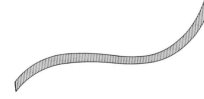

254 2 pieces for the stem

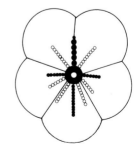

255 When joining is completed beaded lines are sewn to the front of the flower to resemble the lines on a pansy. The edges are pinstuck

A violet or heartsease

This pincushion was immensely popular and considered suitable as a gift for 'a young man'. It is of no practical use.

To make the pincushion
Two pieces of card should be cut from each shape and covered with thin violet-coloured silk. Taffeta ribbon is very suitable. The lower half sometimes is covered with yellow silk for a heartsease.

These joining stitches are covered with beaded sequins sewn on with purple silk, and the edges pinstuck with beads.

It is then ready to be given away.

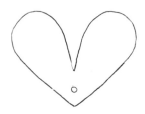 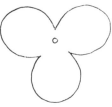

256 Two shapes are used, one for the top half, and one for the lower petals. Small holes should be pierced in each

257 The two halves of each piece are then joined separately with oversewing on the right side

258 The top and bottom sections are then joined by sewing through the pierced holes in each, taking the thread over and behind the angles of the front piece

Re-covering

Silver-mounted, and other similar pincushions, often have needed to be re-covered, and been discarded for their shabby appearance on this account. The original cover of most of the cushions, and certainly those in silver mounts, was blue velvet and this material looks well with silver.

If the mount is hollow as usually is the case, with the swan and frog as examples, the worn cushion should be removed, and any loose sawdust or other filling thrown away, after sorting out needles and so on, which may have worked into it.

A new cushion to fit inside can be made by making a bag of velvet firmly filled with sheep's wool or ravellings, to the appropriate shape and size.

A small amount of adhesive inside the base of the mount should be enough to fix the new cushion in place.

Other mounts can be re-cushioned in this way also, whether they are of basket work, ornamental china, enamel or other materials.

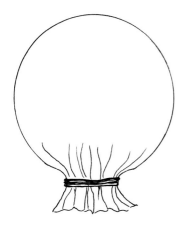

259 The opening of the bag should be tied tightly with strong thread

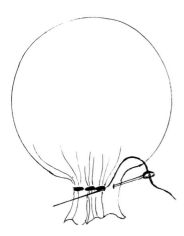

260 Alternatively the fold may be gathered in and Back stitched with firmly drawn stitches

261 A nineteenth-century swan with a temporary pincushion

Some small pincushions, once made for purses or pockets, and others which were among the fittings of workboxes, have outer covers of ivory, mother-of-pearl, bone or silver, as well as Tonbridge Ware and various woods, and are worth renewing when the cushion is worn out.

262 An ivory workbox pincushion finished with blue ribbon

263 A mother of pearl pocket pincushion finished with red ribbon

Ivory, shell and bone covers are drilled at the edges with small holes for sewing, so to renew the pad all old threads and other remains should be removed, especially needles which have worked inside, and the covers washed with luke-warm soapy water.

A pad for a round cushion can be made by rolling a narrow strip of flannel or thin felt (p. 21) until it is of the same circumference as the covers. For other shapes, like butterflies (14), wheel-barrows, bellows and many more, the pad should be made of felt or layers of wool (p. 21) trimmed to the shape of the covers.

To re-join the covers, they should be sewn together by stitching with a coloured silk, to match the finishing ribbon. The needle should be tested for size first, since if it is too thick it will split the holes.

The stitches should be taken through the pad from a hole on one cover, to the opposite hole on the other, all round the cushion. Then a second journey should be made, covering the spaces left the first time round. (See Fig. 264.)

To finish, the edges of the pad are covered with a ribbon, usually red, and tied in a bow.

Covers made of leather, wood, Tonbridge Ware (p. 14) silver and other metal, are usually stuck to the cushion pad and no holes for sewing are made in them.

Layers of thin felt stitched together, or one piece of thick felt should be used. The covers should be coated evenly on the back with a good adhesive like Bostik, and, when stuck to both sides of the pad, the pincushion should be left under a weight, not too heavy, until it is quite dry.

264

Sources for supplies

As such small amounts of material and trimming are needed, usually the piece-bag will supply enough for both. These can be supplemented by others from Jumble Sales, second-hand shops, open markets and other market stalls. Fent shops in the north of England, remnant counters in dress and furnishing stores and 'Oddment' baskets in haberdashery departments are places where anything can be found.

Shopping by post

Because of the uncertainty of prices being constant, enquiries in writing with a stamped addressed envelope are advisable, when shopping by post is necessary.

Transfer pattern sheets nos 113 and 108, can be obtained this way from The Dorset Federation of Women's Institutes, Princes Street, Dorchester, Dorset.

Patchwork template price and pattern sheets from The Moat Wool Co., 34 Parliament Street, Harrogate, Yorkshire.

Materials and threads for embroidery from Mrs Mary Allen, Turnditch, Derbyshire.

Beads and Sequins can be bought from Ells and Farrier, 5 Princes Street, London W1.

266 Ebony purse pincushion with
a silver initial finished with grey
velvet ribbon

265 A white leather pincushion
finished with red velvet ribbon

To finish, a ribbon of silk or velvet should be tied round to cover the
edges of the pad and tied in a neat bow.